MW01617719

# East of the Slash

# EAST OF THE SLASH

*By*

Wade S. Wineman, Jr.

OK PUBLISHING CO.
Greenville, Mississippi

Manufactured in the United States of America
Designed by Robin Wineman Newton

ISBN 0-9655290-0-2

Library of Congress Catalog Card Number 96-92807

OK Publishing Co.
Greenville, Mississippi

# DEDICATION

This work is dedicated to the memory of Wade S. Wineman, Sr. (1921-1994). Through him, his young son was introduced to a creature that his father loved, the world's quintessential game animal. Had he not done so, these memoirs would never have been penned.

# Contents

*Acknowledgements* ... i
*Foreword* ... ii
Ship Island ... 1
OK Bird ... 7
A Shot in the Dark ... 17
Old Timers ... 25
Winn ... 25
Roman ... 32
Jay ... 36
Gearing Up ... 43
Lynched by a Hen ... 49
The Big Mouth of Big Bend ... 55
Going in Circles ... 63
The Hant of Paw Paw Ridge ... 67
The Party Line ... 81
Up Periscope! ... 87
Getting Some ZZZs ... 95
Drilling for Gobblers ... 105
1987—What A Year! ... 109
The Kind Of Problem I'd Like to Have ... 109
Umbrella Feathers ... 113
The Sultan of The Slough ... 118
Fall Can Be Fabulous ... 122
Turkey Hunters 'Tween Twelve and Twenty ... 129
Turkeys on the Tip ... 133
Bully of the Woods ... 141
Temperamental Torrents ... 151
Onion Rings and Other Habits ... 165
Streakers ... 171
Walking The Talk ... 177
Sitters vs. Walkers ... 183
Gobbler Calls are for the Birds ... 191
He Had a Field Day ... 199
East of the Slash ... 207

# ACKNOWLEDGEMENTS

Without the tireless assistance of many friends and family members this work would never have come to fruition. A list of major contributors to the effort includes my wife, Becky, who patiently supported me while I spent many late nights and weekends at my office writing, and who proofread my manuscripts. And my mother, Nancy, who also proofread the manuscripts and provided needed moral support. I also extend special thanks to my sister, Robin, for her splendid dustjacket design.

I am also indebted to my cousin, attorney Whit Rayner, who guided me through the legal maze associated with getting this work published; to Ted Roman, of American Printing Co., for his advice and for providing the necessary printing services; to Gene Smith, retired editor of *Turkey Call* magazine for his editorial advice; and to Billy Brookshire, for inspiring me to begin the hunting journal that led to these stories.

# FOREWORD

Most of us have a place out there somewhere that's magical—our own little Oz on the other side of the rainbow. I know people who own houses and condominiums on the beach. I know others who own vacation homes in Colorado. And I know a bunch of folks who just rent places when they take their families on vacation to the beach every summer. When they're back home, most of these folks occasionally daydream during the course of the year about the next trip back to their earthly paradises.

The people I know who fantasize the most, however, are hunters. Few of them spend an entire day without having at least one thought about their woods or their hunting cabin flicker through their synapses. This is the way it is with me, except I have a double-dose of it. My mind wanders at some point during each day, without exception, to the woods where I hunt, and always thereafter to fantasies about wild turkeys strutting before me in a glade, in a full shaft of sunlight, or some similar scene.

When writers are asked why they wrote their books, most respond with the cliche that they had something inside them and they felt compelled to release it. Notwithstanding a lack of originality, this is precisely what I experienced. The island where I've hunted all of my life, and its most cherished resident, the wild turkey, have been special to me for as long as I can remember, and I determined at an early age that I would have to tell others about it. That's precisely why, some 25 years ago, I started keeping a log of all my turkey-hunting experiences there.

The focus of this book is not intended to be on imparting what minuscule wisdom I might have obtained in my years of turkey hunting to other hunters for the enhancement of their skills. Rather, it's probably best described as the recollections, sometimes nostalgic, sometimes humorous, of one who has stalked the world's finest creature for a lot of years at one of the world's loveliest sites.

In the very first chapter the reader will discover this extraordinary place. In the second chapter he will be introduced to its most celebrated full-time resident, and thereafter to the various people who intermittently trod the fair soil there.

The anecdotes within are totally factual. Many are based on actual accounts taken directly from the author's personal journal. The individuals mentioned and names used are also genuine and have not been changed to protect the innocent.

# EAST OF THE SLASH

## Chapter 1

# SHIP ISLAND

"Shoo Fly Bar," "Mhoon Bend," "Montezuma Towhead," "Whiskey Island," "Rowdy Bend." These are only a few of the many peculiar names you'll find when you scan a Mississippi River navigation map. Some of the most fascinating things about the river are the names of landmarks such as these found along its banks.

Whiskey Island was so named because a luckless barge supposedly ran aground and spilled its spirituous contents there. The origins of most of these landmark names, however, have long been forgotten and are now lost in antiquity.

One landmark possessing a name of forgotten origin is a small island known as Ship Island, which is just across the river from Whiskey Island in Tunica County, Mississippi.

Ship Island and "OK Bar," Ship Island's lower end, were both mentioned in "Gone are the Honkers" and other stories by Nash Buckingham. Legendary Beaverdam Lake, the setting of many other tales by Mr. Buck, is only three miles east of Ship Island.

Ship Island, like many other islands along the Mississippi River, is an island only when the river is at high stages. With the exception of annual spring, and occasional winter, high waters, the island can be easily accessed by land during the year.

Ship Island formed as an accretion occurring when the river slowly shifted west from its 1835 meander line near the little hamlet of Austin. It was at Ship Island, across from Austin, where the steamboat *Pennsylvania* exploded in 1858 with the loss of 150 lives, including Henry Clemens, the brother of Samuel Clemens (Mark Twain). Twain later wrote about this disaster in his book, *Life on the Mississippi.*

In the mid-1970s, while my dad and faithful longtime employee O. L. Actwood were surveying the south boundary of our Ship-Island tract, their compass needle was pulled wildly off line on the west bank of Old River Lake, near the 1835 river meander line.

Professional surveyors will tell you that such a strong magnetic attraction is usually caused by an underground iron object of enormous size. We always speculated that the source of the attraction might be a steam boiler or other large iron object from the wreckage of the *Pennsylvania,* which would have been long-since silted over by alluvial deposits.

My family has owned a portion of Ship Island since the early 1900s. My great-grandfather and his sons left Gates, Tennessee, in 1896 and came to Greenville, Mississippi, to set up a lumber mill. They purchased timberland upstream, so logs could be floated down the river to the mill. The mill itself closed in 1929, but they decided to keep the land in

Tunica County.

The Mississippi River country of those days was a howling wilderness, and the pioneers who lived along it were a rugged breed. Timber tracts along the river were often located on roadless, isolated points of land, miles from the nearest town. Gas outboard motors were rare, and four-wheel-drive vehicles were non existent.

In that era a hunting trip was a monumental undertaking— almost the equivalent of embarking on the Oregon Trail. It required serious commitment to get there, and once you were there you stayed a while.

My grandfather Bob and his friends were avid goose hunters, and camped out on a houseboat for a week at a time when they hunted on the river. I have some old photos of them on the boat, which was used as a home base from which side trips to remote stretches of the river originated.

An interesting procedure was required for my grandmother to send a message to my grandfather when he was working on another tract he had in Tunica County, on Whiskey Island. She began the process by phoning the desk clerk at the Marie Hotel in Tunica, and the clerk gave the message to the mail carrier when he delivered mail to the hotel. When the carrier ran his rural route, he relayed the message to a commercial fisherman who lived on the bank of the river at Mhoon Landing. When the fisherman later crossed the river to check his nets, he would boat up Whitehall Run-Out and Whiskey Chute, and leave the message at the cabin of the caretaker on the island, Harvey Chipman.

The commercial fisherman was one of the few people on the river at that time who owned a gas motor. Bob also hired the fisherman to transfer him across the river to inspect logging on the island. On one of these inspection trips, he finished his work a day earlier than expected. Of course, there were no phones on the island, and patience wasn't a trait Granddaddy Bob was blessed with. Instead of waiting a day on the fisherman, he packed his suitcase and asked Harvey to take him down to the river.

*Grandfather Bob Wineman at his floating hunting camp on the Mississippi River ca. 1920*

In those days it was common to find whole trees, with roots and limbs intact, floating down the Mississippi River. The river was constantly changing course and cutting the unrevetted banks, and frequently several acres of land, trees and all, would collapse into the brutal torrent.

Bob and Harvey looked until they found a tree of

adequate diameter bobbing against the riverbank. Granddad slung his suitcase and an oar up into the branches, straddled the bole of the tree, and held on while Harvey used a long pole to shove the whole makeshift craft out into the current.

Somehow, using natural river dynamics and the oar, Granddaddy Bob maneuvered his way across to the opposite bank 11 miles downstream, and made landfall at Fox Island. From there he walked a mile through the woods and across the levee to the Mangum farm, where he hitched a ride back to his car at the fisherman's cabin.

It's a different world now. Massive bridges have replaced the old ferries that once crossed the mighty stream. They span the river and facilitate vehicular travel from one side to the other. Four-wheel-drive vehicles of every imaginable size and shape, and capacious river crafts with large engines make accessible the most hidden reaches of the river.

Still, surprisingly large pockets of wilderness survive today between the protection levees that parallel the river. In some areas, unbroken tracts of timber stretch for miles, encompassing tens of thousands of acres, an ecosystem perfectly conceived by the Creator to accommodate our honored subject, his majesty *Meleagris gallopavo silvestris,* the Eastern wild turkey.

## Chapter 2

# OK Bird

Tunica County, Mississippi, is smack in the middle of the range of the eastern subspecies of the wild turkey. At the turn of the century, Tunica County, as well as the entire Mississippi Delta region, remained heavily forested and wild turkeys were almost as common as woodpeckers there.

There were no such things as bag limits and game management, and market hunters and game-hogs methodically slaughtered the birds.

Apparently, the most devastating method of eradication was the "bait trench." The method involved a shooter positioning himself on one end of a baited corn trench, waiting until an entire flock fed into the trench, lining up as many necks as possible, and spraying them down with an open-bore shotgun. Entire local turkey populations could be exterminated in short order that way.

This type of thing occurred with disturbing frequency, and it, combined with the loss of deep-forest habitat, served to totally eradicate the wild turkey from many areas within its original range. Supposedly, by the 1930s the turkey had disappeared in Mississippi, except for small areas near Meridian, in the Pascagoula River bottoms near the gulf coast, and in Tunica and northern Coahoma counties.

Some Tunica County locals say that the reason for the turkey being saved there was because of the Perry family. The Perrys have owned timberland in the county, north of Ship Island, for many decades. They have acquired a well-deserved reputation for aggressively guarding their timberland against trespass.

Some of the more colorful accounts of their dealings with poachers have become legends. Many locals believe that, because of the fear instilled in the poaching public by the Perrys, a good seed flock of turkeys was preserved while the rest of the state's flocks were being wiped out.

Tunica County was also blessed with having, for many years, probably the best game warden in the state, Cliff Thornton. "Mr. Cliff" had an easy-going style that was disarming, but he wouldn't hesitate to arrest his own grandma.

He would do the dirty work, like staking out a place overnight, but he was most accomplished in the public relations aspect of the job. He was usually one of the first ones to hear when something irregular occurred in the county.

The only time I ever remember somebody on our club running afoul of Mr. Cliff was back in the '50s, when one of our club members couldn't resist the impulse to shoot two gobblers in one day in the spring season. The club hadn't been in existence long, and that was probably the first time anybody had accomplished such a feat, so the proud outlaw boasted to a group of local members on the adjacent hunting club.

A couple of days later, while doing public relations work over coffee at the Blue & White Cafe, Cliff heard the rumor. He received a prompt confession when he confronted the surprised suspect the next weekend.

Cliff's wide network of friends and informers kept him constantly online in the information highway of that day, and undoubtedly this also protected many turkeys from the poacher's gun.

After World War II, when the modern hunting boom began, there were people in Washington County, my home county, who considered a wild turkey to be about as real as a Phoenix. Most people had never heard of a wild turkey, and few had ever seen one.

Prior to World War II, hunting along the river was predominantly a pursuit of the proverbial "river rat." People worked six full days a week then, and the country was in the oppressive grip of the Great Depression. Times were different. Leisure time was limited, and wild game had been mostly eradicated in earlier years.

When things stabilized after the war, new hunting clubs began to lease much of the land between the levee and the Mississippi River. Almost all of this land was in timber and destined to remain that way due to flood hazard.

Most of the new hunting clubs were long on whiskey and short on deer and turkeys. It would be the late 1950s or early 1960s before most of them would have significant populations of either of the latter. Many areas without wild turkey populations were stocked with turkeys trapped in

Tunica County during those years.

At the north end of Ship Island in Tunica County, Charlie Fortner operated a little back woods fishing camp on Tunica Cutoff Lake, about ¾ mile from the levee down a narrow, muddy woods road. Dad let him stay on the island rent-free, in return for watching out for fires and poaching and the like.

I have a dim recollection from childhood of Fortner's place, a memory of a black fox squirrel that he had trained to come up to his cabin. Charlie fit the mold of the river rat well. He was a rough-hewn pioneer type who, to a great extent, lived off the bounties of nature. Rough though he was, this hale character will always have a hallowed place in my memory, because he was the one that introduced my father to wild-turkey hunting. From the time that Dad returned from the war, Charlie had been telling him fanciful tales about Ship Island's abundant turkey population.

Until he stopped cotton farming in 1951, Dad had been unable to turkey hunt. He had been a prolific duck hunter, dove hunter, and bass fisherman all his life, but cotton farming did not dovetail with turkey hunting. The turkey season occurred at precisely the time of peak preparations for cotton planting. After he stopped farming, Dad started listening more closely to Charlie's stories. In the spring of 1953, he decided to give the new sport a try.

Dad arrived at Fortner's cabin the afternoon before his first hunt, so the two could draw up a battle plan. Since the Cutoff was swollen with spring flood water, it was decided that Fortner would pilot them three miles down the black lake with his small john boat and gas motor. Charlie explained that he would locate some turkey gobblers by calling on his homemade box call, but didn't give a whole lot more in the way of details.

They hit the lake bank at the same latitude of The "Slash," an old depression low enough to commonly hold river backwater in the spring of the year. They stepped onto the ridge between the lake and The Slash, gathered their breath, and waited for first light. When dawn came, Charlie scratched on the box, and some of the most raucous sounds imaginable came forth.

Cacophonous though the sounds were, Dad heard gobbling begin in front of him and extend, domino style, down The Slash in both directions, until it was out of hearing range. Fortner whispered to him, "Wawk up to Th' Slash, wayd on owt thar and shoot wun off a lim fuh ya sef, den shoot anuder wun fuh me, too."

Bug-eyed, Dad obeyed the frontiersman, and things went according to plan. Dad craned his neck around carefully until he found a longbeard, as he had been instructed, then took aim, and touched off a shot. Down through the limbs crashed the huge bird until he cannonballed in the knee-deep water and started flopping. Dad gleefully sloshed through the water, retrieved the soaked bird, and returned to the bank of The Slash.

A moment or so after Dad had laid the longbeard down, the string of gobbling resumed. Dad looked slightly to the left of the first gobbler's perch and, to his amazement, saw another gobbler, just as huge and just as bearded as the first. Remembering Fortner's words, he tiptoed back into the water, raised his shotgun, and fired again. His second shot apparently went awry, because the gobbler flew off.

Dad returned to where the grinning Fortner was

*Wade S. Wineman, Sr., with gobbler taken in 1956.*

standing and apologized for missing one of the obviously "dumb" birds. Of course, this was of no special concern to Fortner, since he had been killing the things for years and knew he was going to kill a boat full later that spring.

Tunica County birds had received little hunting pressure over the years, and many tales of dumb gobblers would ensue during the early days of the hunting club that would soon be organized.

Each time I reminisce about those early days, and review my own hunting journal of later hunts, I'm surprised when I remember again how brief the dumb-turkey period was. After only five or six years, the birds were embarrassing everybody.

When the news about Dad's experience with Fortner made it back to his hometown of Greenville, it piqued the interest of two of his friends, Dr. Eustace Winn and Raymond Kimble. At the same time, a group of Tunica County locals were discussing the formation of a new hunting club on the Seabrook and Bailey lands adjacent to our Ship-Island tract.

A plan was adopted to unite our land with theirs, resulting in the formation of a 4,600-acre club, the "OK Hunting Club." Dad and his two Greenville friends were the only members of the new organization who were not from Tunica County.

The three Greenville hunters meant business when it came to hunting, especially turkey hunting. For most of the years in the early 1950s, the Mississippi wild turkey season ran for only about 10 or 12 days in early April. Frequently, the Greenville three would remain at Tunica for the entire season.

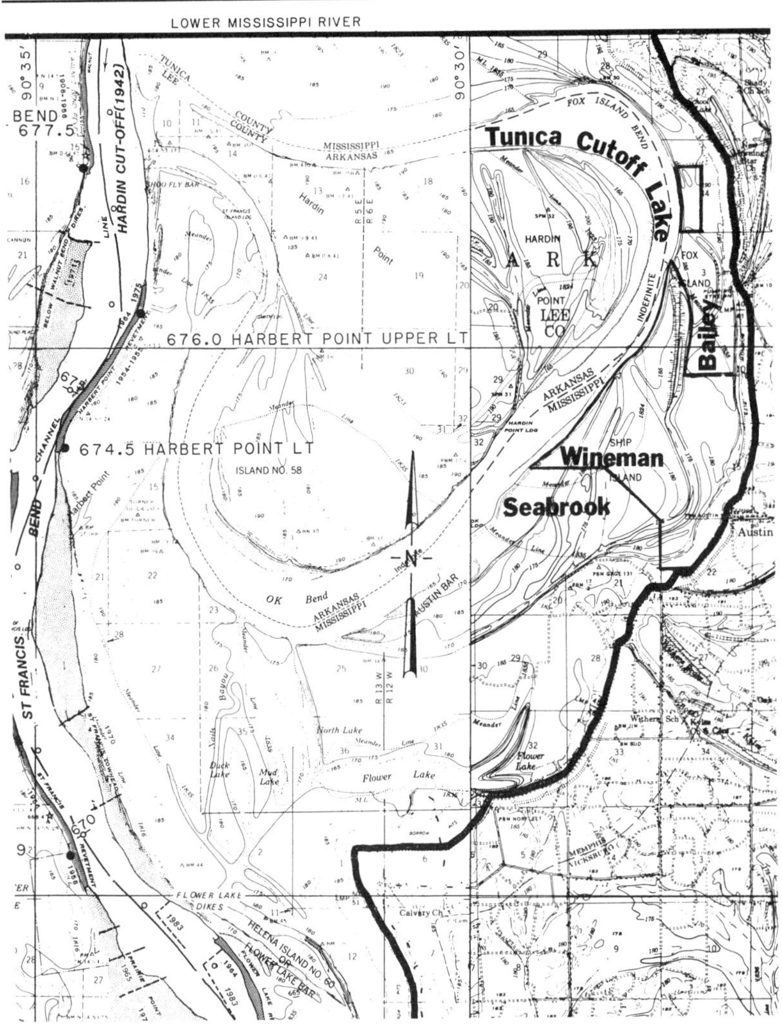


*Location of the OK Hunting Club—on the Wineman, Bailey, and Seabrook Tracts.*

A splendid arrangement it was to be for the three of them, for they discovered that most of the local hunters were disposed to camping out at their cabin and going after Wild Turkey in a glass rather than wild turkeys in the woods. This meant that, for as long as these three tracts of land were combined, from 1955 through 1968, the three Greenville members and their guests had the run of practically the whole 4,600 acres during spring turkey season, resulting in one of the best acres-per-hunter ratios along the river.

This isn't to say that the Greenville bunch had glasses of buttermilk and went to bed at eight every night when they came up to the OK Club to hunt. Cherubic they were not. In those early days, while most of the Tunica boys gathered at Seabrook's small cabin, the Greenville boys chose to stay at Sam Wasserman's Tunica Motel. The motel had 16 rooms, and many are the weekends that I remember Greenville hunters and their guests filling up a dozen or more of the rooms. No hunting camp out in the hinterlands was ever more raucous. Glasses containing mysterious liquids littered the tables at the all-night poker games in the smoke-filled rooms of the motel.

My own dad wasn't a gambler, however, and I remember being irritated at him because he refused to let me stay up late and watch the games. Instead he was focused entirely on the hunt, and we retired early each night, to the sounds of tinkling glasses and laughter two or three doors down the stoop.

When this group descended on the famous Blue & White Cafe in Tunica for supper, it was an adventure every time. One of the loyal waitresses at the cafe had brown hair with just a hint of red in it, and was especially soft-spoken. I can still see Kimble bellowing like a camel across the room to her, "Red,... Red,... come here, Red." He called her Red from then on, and she never stopped blushing about it.

The Blue & White had the best onion rings you could find anywhere. The men used to tease the young 'uns about coming to Tunica to go "onion ring" hunting, but onion rings were only a minor motivation. As important to us as onion rings, the poker room, or the candy our fathers pacified us with in the woods, was the mystical allure of an almost-supernatural bird.

## Chapter 3

# A Shot in the Dark

It was opening day of the spring season, 1955, when my father and Raymond Kimble took Dr. E. H. Winn, Jr., on his first turkey hunt at Ship Island. Dad and Raymond had been hunting buddies for several years. Dr. Winn and Dad had been childhood friends, but had not hunted together for about 15 years, because Winn had been off at medical school.

Dad and Raymond were so alike that it was hard to picture them hunting together. They both had a proclivity to issue expletives upon the least provocation, and each presumed his own way to be the only way to get something done. Often I saw them growling and cursing each other while repairing an outboard motor or something, but I always knew that, in spite of it all, they had a real fondness for each other.

The two had been tantalizing Dr. Winn for months with talk of the glut of wild turkeys at Ship Island, and it was all they could do to restrain him from opening the season up a week early. Prior to opening morning they sought to imbue him with the collective wisdom gleaned from their two years of hunting: how to hoot like an owl to make turkeys gobble, how to operate a Lynch box call, how to identify the sexes, and so forth. The one thing that was drummed into the doctor's mind most was that it was a fate worse than death to suffer the embarrassment of accidentally shooting a hen turkey.

The usual spring flood was on at season's start that year. The two tutors escorted their neophyte pupil to the hunt early on opening morning. After the five-mile drive to the levee, they off-loaded their john boat by a crystalline moon into the river backwater lapping at the levee's base. After loading the boat, they began sculling it across the levee borrow pits, and then down a flooded, narrow logging trail that was arched by overhanging limbs.

Several minutes after entering the flooded trail, Kimble, who was in the bow, suddenly noticed a bulky, dark mass silhouetted in the predawn moonlight on a limb above them. He studied the object for a few seconds and silently concluded that it had to be a gobbler.

He quietly withdrew his sculling paddle from the murky water, turned around in the boat, and whispered excitedly to the surgeon, "There's one on that limb right above us. Shoot him, Winn!"

As instructed, the surgeon slowly began to shoulder his Model 12. On the way up, he heard Dad's voice murmur from the stern of the boat, "Better make sure he has a beard, Winn." The harsh, preseason admonition about hen shooting had made the thought of such an act anathema to Winn. His weapon began to descend as slowly as it had risen.

Kimble, with more assertiveness, reissued the order, "Shoot, him, Winn. Now!" Again, the Model 12 rose, and again the caveat from behind him was whispered, "Make sure he's a gobbler, Winn." The gun was again reluctantly lowered by Winn, who by then was trembling with anxiety.

After the second round, Kimble could stand no more. "#$&! it, Winn, you son of a &@@$#, shoot the @#$&$@# turkey!" After Kimble's eruption, the dark mass on the limb decided it could also stand no more and sailed off with a beard so immense that, even in the dark, it looked like a fire hose. Dad was berated by Kimble and Winn for years after that for botching the doctor's first hunt.

*Four by Four*
*L. to r., Dr. Chas. Harrison, Walter Roman, Raymond Kimble, Dr. E.H. Winn, Jr.*

The old OK Hunting Club was accorded a measure of fame with the issuance of the April, 1960, Field & Stream magazine, in a story entitled "Boss Gobbler." The authors credited for the story were my father and Robert Price, but Price was the one who actually did the writing.

Bob Price was a free lance outdoor writer whose real job was field man for the National Cotton Council, a job which required considerable travel and afforded him the opportunity to cover a lot of hunting and fishing territory. My uncle, Walter Rayner, also worked for the Cotton Council, and he occasionally came to Ship Island to hunt turkeys with us.

Walter originated the idea and made arrangements for Price to come for a weekend to do a story on wild-turkey hunting in Tunica County. Stories on turkey hunting were rare in those days. There were few turkey hunters because there were so few wild turkeys in most places.

Price interviewed everyone in camp, took photos, and participated in the hunts. Since he didn't know the first thing about turkey hunting, he spent most of his time with Dad, Kimble, and Winn, because they supposedly knew more about it than anybody else in camp. After Price left, the three could hardly wait until the article was published, because they were all sure they would have prominent places in the story.

The long-awaited issue of Field & Stream hit the newsstands in mid-March, right before the start of the 1960 spring season. I remember the day clearly. Dad brought home six or eight copies, and we read the article immediately.

The story had been contrived by Bob, and was a sentimental tale about a father who wanted to call up a mythical boss gobbler for his young son.

The story told how, when the father had finally lured the bird within range, the son was asleep in the blind and the father was forced to take the shot himself. It was all fictitious, except for the names of the people and the terrain features involved.

When I reached the end of the story, I knew something was missing, and it finally struck me. Nowhere in the entire story did it mention the names of Kimble or Winn. The only names mentioned were Dad's, mine, and my uncle Walter's. Price had even included color photos of the three of us, including one of Walter and a fine gobbler he had killed that weekend.

Well, you never heard cussing as abrasive as Kimble's when he discovered the omissions, and my father was chided by both him and Winn for decades after they read Price's powder-puff story.

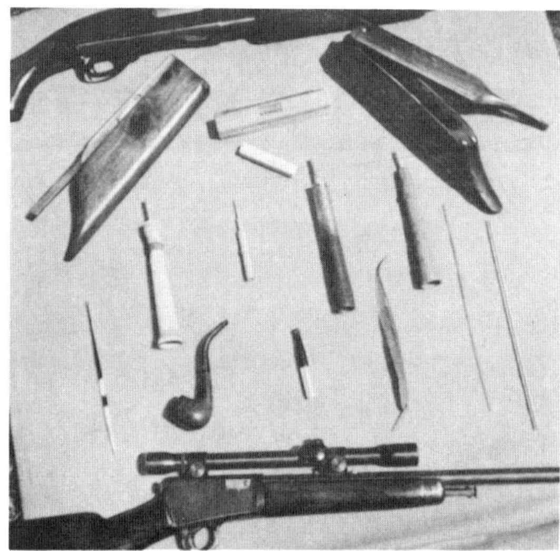
Turkey calls: some you rattle, some you scrape, some you blow, some you suck. With all, you hope

# Boss Gobbler

By WADE WINEMAN, SR.
With ROBERT E. PRICE

LITTLE Wade Wineman, Jr., in his eleventh year, was out to bag his first wild turkey. If things went well, it was to be a very special turkey—the boss gobbler of Cottonwood Flats. I was along on the hunt to call the boss in for my son and to try to outwit the old tom with the techniques I'd developed during many years of turkey hunting. It was mid-April and our range was the O.K. Hunting Club, which lies between the Mississippi River and the levee, in the northwestern corner of Mississippi.

I was proud of my young son, for he was an apt pupil. Already he had busted doves and mallards on the wing. As the time approached for the gobbler hunt he had been seized with turkey fever. No wonder. Under the expert tutoring of Walter "Box" Rayner, his favorite uncle and one of our companions on the 2-day hunt, he was becoming a fanatic on the subject of our greatest bird.

Wade and I were within a quarter mile of the roost when the first redbird cut loose with its shrill salute to the dawn. At any moment now the old battle-scarred warrior might blast forth his raucous challenge to all the tom turkeys in the flats, daring even a peep out of them. "De boss gobbler am de hugest, fiercest, and smahtest ole tu'key I ever seed," Pegleg Bowman had told me. "He don't 'low no other gobblers paying co't to he big flock of lady folk and he won't let no hunter get nowhar nigh him. Yas, suh, hit'll take a mite of doing to outsmaht dat ole tom."

Pegleg was a hunter who would know a smart old turkey. So, all in all, it seemed unlikely we'd hear any sound from the boss that would betray his position. There was a chance that in spite of his large harem the black-bearded sultan might reply to the ardent yelp of a hen. But most probably, I thought, he would resent and answer the war cry of another gobbler boldly invading his range.

I quietly moved a dry limb and helped Wade find a comfortable seat in the windfall we had earlier selected for cover. After donning a pair of olive-drab gloves to hide my white skin, I raised the call box above my head and swept it down sharply, shaking it hard. The stick of chalk inside rattled loudly, and the chalked lid rasped back and forth across the top. This kind of call is the best imitation I know of the trumpeting, spine-tingling blast

40

*The infamous 1960 **Field & Stream** article*

Little Wade watches attentively for action as I stroke a yelp out of my box

Three's no crowd when one is the boss gobbler, boss no more. Young Wade is wide awake now—but it wasn't always so

**When you take your young son out for his first wild turkey you want him to get the biggest old gobbler on the roost. Maybe that's where you make your mistake**

of an amorous tom turkey. Tensely I awaited results.

It worked! The boss gobbler bellowed his defiance and we heard the thudding *whoompf, whoompf, whoompf* of wingbeats as a heavy body crashed through the foliage from one perch to another, followed by the barely discernible swish of his glide to the ground. The king of the swamp was coming down from his throne to join battle.

We had made contact, which is vitally important. But it might be minutes, hours, or forever before the kill. Wade would wait tensely, remembering all the things I had taught him. He knew that the wild gobbler is the largest, shrewdest, spookiest, and—consequently—the greatest prize of all the American game birds. Pushed hard, he may tramp over you if you're sitting or standing stone-still. You may even flush him unexpectedly in dense cover or from behind a ridge. But you'll never, never successfully stalk him once he's spotted you, for he has X-ray eyes, radar ears, and a four-barrel carburetor.

Yesterday morning the fates had been against us. At the crack of dawn I cupped my hands over my mouth and hooted like an owl—my favorite (*Continued on page* 126)

Box Rayner, Wade's uncle and turkey tutor, got his bird when it gobbled back at a river-boat whistle

41

*The infamous 1960* ***Field & Stream*** *article (continued)*

## Chapter 4

# OLD TIMERS

### WINN

Stories of Dr. Eustace Winn abound in the lore of the old OK Hunting Club. Several involved boats. Because of the frequency and extent of flooding along the Mississippi River, club members often had to boat down Tunica Cutoff Lake to reach the isolated ridges they planned to hunt.

Ship Island is on the outside of a bend in the lake, what formerly had been old "OK" bend of the river itself before it was cut off from the main channel by the Corps of Engineers. The outside of a bend is always where the "caving bank" is, where land sloughed off when the river was active, leaving a steep bank and abrupt dropoffs into deep water.

Doc Winn is probably the most unselfish individual I have ever known. The kind that always tries to beat everybody to the sink to wash the dishes after supper. The one who always shoves everybody out of the way to get to the checkout-counter to pay for breakfast at the cafe. He is good at these kinds of maneuvers because he is physically as stout as a grizzly bear. His aggressive, unselfish nature endears him to many folks, but it has also caused him problems at times.

One such occasion occurred in the black, starless predawn of a spring morning, when the river stage was high. Dr. Winn, his son Hal, and Dad and I were racing down the lake in Dr. Winn's brand-new ski boat, trying to beat the crack of dawn to the Outhouse Ridge. We landed on the steep bank of the ridge, and, before anyone else could move, the surgeon put the boat in neutral and leapt to the front deck to tie off the boat. He was wearing chest waders, but misjudged the degree of slope of the lake bank. When he stepped off the front of the boat, he plunged into the water like a hippo in the Congo, leaving in view only his bobbing, Jones-style cap. When he surfaced, the ensuing thrashing and commotion elicited such a riotous response from the rest of us that the turkeys shut up and didn't gobble all day.

A couple of years later, the good doctor had to terminate a hunt early to meet someone back in town. The spring flood was on, and he was in his ski boat again. He was running late when he returned to the boat, and hurriedly began to load up his gear. Without thinking, he un-slung his prized Model 12 Winchester, 3-inch magnum, 12 gauge, and gently set it on the roof of the boat. He dropped his other gear on the floor of the boat, and climbed in. When he hit the ignition switch, there was no response from the outboard motor. He turned the key several more times, to no avail. Feeling the stress of time even more, he decided to abandon the electric starter and hand-crank the engine. He impatiently shoved the throttle full forward and walked to the back of the boat. Just as he yanked the starter-cord, a fleeting recollection of the gun on the roof zipped through his mind, but it was too late. The 80-horse motor resuscitated on the first pull, instantly propelling the boat forward. Luckily, it slammed into a willow tree before it could reach full speed. As Doc was thrown to the floor of the boat, he caught in the corner of his eye a glimpse of the Model 12 whistling off the roof into the 15-foot-deep water.

We also used to hunt on Whiskey Island, a river island across from Ship Island. When we hunted there, we put our boats in at Mhoon Landing (where north Mississippi's first casino would later locate), and cross the Father of Waters to the island for a two- or three-day hunt.

One such hunt occurred in the spring of 1961. Our lodging on the island was at the old Harvey Chipman cabin, which sat above flood-level on an old mound pushed up in pioneer times.

We departed Mhoon Landing, crossed Old Muddy, and motored up Whitehall Lake runout until we reached Whiskey Chute. Then up the chute we came, and what a fight it was, the chute gorged with logs, privet, button willow and willow trees. The outboard motors sounded almost like jackhammers as they struggled to propel us up the flooded, narrow depression.

Dr. Winn, at one point, managed to steer his boat into a particularly tight place, kind of like a catfish working himself into a slat-basket. Once he was stuck, he began trying to back into more open water, but the situation continued to worsen. He sawed back and sawed forward, sometimes only inches at a time, becoming increasingly frustrated with each attempt.

At precisely the height of Doc's frustration, Dad calmly asked him, "Winn, do you want me to run the boat and get us out of this mess?" You couldn't have energized Doc more if you had stuck a red-hot poker up his butt.

With Dad's question still echoing in his head, Dr. Winn decided to use brute force. He backed hard into the scant opening behind the bulky boat, then shifted to forward and came down full throttle. The craft smashed through a screen of biomass like a charging water buffalo, then slammed into a willow tree and climbed right up its side.

It's no exaggeration that, on impact, one of the six-gallon fuel cans at the stern shot like a hockey puck all the way to the bow, luckily inflicting no injuries enroute.

Dr. Winn piloted the same boat for several years after that, and every time I saw the concave nose at its bow, I remembered the experience with a chuckle.

Dr. Winn's misfortunes continued that same weekend. After hunting all morning on the first day, he and Walter Roman began scouting the ridge on the north side of Whiskey Chute in the afternoon. Roman went west along the north bank of the chute, while Doc went due north.

They agreed to rendezvous at the boat at dusk and return to the cabin, which was across and down the chute a short distance. Walter got back at dusk, as planned. Darkness fell. He waited an hour, then two, then three, and still Dr. Winn didn't show up.

Thinking that a search party might be advisable, he came back across the chute to the cabin for help. After a short discussion, it was decided that two hunters would return to the point of Doc's departure, continue to wait, and fire a gun periodically so that Winn, if lost, could come to the sound.

*L. to r., Wade Wineman, Sr., Harvey Chipman, Dr. E. H. Winn*
*Whiskey Island hunt, April, 1960*

*Dr. E. H. Winn, after a successful hunt in 1959*

At midnight, Doc appeared, looking like Jack the Ripper's last victim. His parka was shredded to ribbons, and rivulets of sweat were draining down his face and neck.

He explained, "After listening for a gobbler to fly up to roost, I started back after dark. I knew I had to come back south to get to the boat, and I followed my compass faithfully until I broke out into one of Harvey's cotton fields that I recognized, and then knew I was headed wrong. I finally figured out that the luminous dot on the compass was painted on the south arrow instead of the north arrow, like I thought. After I got turned around the right way, I headed back here, but I was a good two miles back in the woods, and had to return in the dark without a flashlight."

Notwithstanding these misadventures, I regard Dr. Winn as one of the premier turkey hunters I have known. Many are the springs that he has filled both Mississippi and Arkansas limits of gobblers. I personally have learned much from him.

There has never been a more tenacious hunter. He is, even today, at age 74, with arthritic knees, always the last hunter to come out of the woods after dark.

He's one of those rare hunters who, upon hearing no gobbling, will sit in a blind (preferably a log blind) for five hours calling on several of his prized old Stribling box calls, and make things happen. It's amazing how many birds he kills that way. Gobblers just seem to eventually materialize before him. It takes a person of immense patience and skill to do that, and he does it better than anyone else I know.

And what a sportsman! He promotes bagging a gobbler "the right way," the most sporting way—no rifle, no limb shooting, no decoy.

## ROMAN

Walter Roman was another of my father's best hunting buddies, and he frequently hunted on the island with us. You didn't have to be an Indian scout to follow Roman's trail in the woods. He loved those small cigars with a plastic mouthpiece on the end of them. He used to come to Tunica with a case of them, and those little white plastic end tips were so easy to see on a logging trail that you could follow his hunting route every day.

Roman holds the distinction of being the only individual to ever have a landmark on Ship Island named for him. Dad had always wanted to have a road running southeast down the ridge east of The Slash, but loggers had never constructed one there. In the bottomland-hardwood forests along the river, almost all of the roads originated as logging trails.

After a morning hunt in the spring of 1968, Dad, Roman, and Roman's son, Ted, opened a new road ¾ of a mile long down the ridge east of The Slash. They did this with a Ford Bronco, pulling a log with a chain through solid woods. That rudimentary path has evolved into a major road on the island, and has been known as the "Roman Road" ever since.

Roman is best described as a "sport"—personable, agreeable, and always willing to help. Many are the fond memories he has provided OK-club hunters.

One of the most famous, and most recounted, tales of the island is the one about Roman's first gobbler. Most of his friends had killed their first turkeys the year before, and he felt the pressure to prove himself. He had worked a gobbler with his Lynch box one morning for two hours, ever since coming-off-the-roost time. Finally luring the gobbler into range, he emptied his 12 gauge, only to see the resilient gobbler run away. Roman, who scaled out at 6-3 and 240, began smashing through the brush in desperate pursuit of the bird. He had seen a wing hanging, and that encouraged him to keep up the chase.

It was a typical spring, with the river backed up into the woods along the edge of the ridge Roman was on. By chance, the wounded bird ran in the direction of the backwater, and Roman began to gain ground. When the gobbler reached the edge of the backwater, it slammed on the brakes and stopped instantly. Roman was like a locomotive under load, unable to stop his 240 pounds as quickly. As he tore past the bird and hit the water, he reflexively reached out with his right hand. He grabbed the sinewy neck, and his fingers took a set as he literally squeezed the life out of the creature. Roman did not emerge from the battle unscathed, however. The gobbler's wings punished him and he was slashed with inch-plus spurs.

After the bird had stopped quivering, Roman couldn't make his hand release the limp neck. His fingers had assumed a kind of rigor mortis, and he had to pry them loose, one at a time.

Roman acquired quite a reputation at our camp for his running ability. On another occasion, he and Dr. Winn were hunting south of the Yellow-Line Road, down on the Seabrook part of the club. They located a large flock early, with several gobblers in it. They moved and called the gobblers from two different positions, but were unsuccessful in luring them to within range. The gobblers were responding well, however, to gobbles made on Dr. Winn's box.

A •• April 2, 1959 THE COMMERCIAL APPEAL, MEMP

*Mid-South Outdoors—*

## From Bullfrogs To Turkeys Keeps Writer On The Move

By HENRY REYNOLDS

When a fellow opens two seasons in less than 12 hours, he's really hustling.

This writer started sticking bullfrogs Tuesday night at 8, grabbed a few winks sleep, then went out after Mississippi wild turkey at 3:30 yesterday morning.

With Lakeview's Fred Miller as a gigging companion, we visited a couple of ponds east of Walls, Miss., Tuesday night and sacked up 20 nice jumpers.

The frogs haven't started bellowing yet and they're not out in force, but those who have ventured out are big boys. We narrowly escaped losing a part of our loot when the frogs found a hole in the gunny sack and slipped out into the bottom of the boat.

It just so happened that the boat was a bit muddy and they couldn't get their jumping mechanism geared up enough to get over the sides. We rounded them all up.

The opening on the gobblers was a wet one. Rain had already splattered the windshield of Casey Jones' station wagon when he picked me up in the wee hours of the morn.

Casey, one of the boating boys from Poplar Kraft, had made arrangements with Henry Lee of Tunica Cutoff to hunt on some land adjoining the boat camp.

**Bags 19-Pounder**

We got into the woods just before daybreak. En route in we flushed one turkey off a roost and stopped to hear one gobble. Other than that, we got nothing but a drenching and returned to the Lee Cafe about 8.

The rain lasted a good hour, then the sun trickled through. We returned to the woods but the turkeys did not appear, although another was heard to gobble.

Wade Wineman of Greenville, Miss., owner of the land Lee has leased, had a hunting party with him. Only one member, Walter Roman, scored. He bagged a 19-pound gobbler about 7:30.

This is the first part of Mississippi's split season. It will continue through April 7. The second season will run from April 13 through April 19.

FOUR IN A ROW—Walter Roman, Greenville Miss., planter, has been hunting wild turkeys only four years but has killed one each season. He bagged his fourth yesterday morning near Tunica Cutoff, where he was a guest of Wade Wineman, Greenville businessman.

—Staff Phot

*Walter Roman's moment of glory in **Memphis Commercial Appeal** article in 1959*

Finally, the two moved for a third time. They spotted the birds far through the woods, and Dr. Winn devised a new strategy. He told Roman to circle wide around the birds and approach through the cane from the west. He would continue to gobble on his box, and Roman could keep them located by their gobbling, while moving into position to ambush them from the cane.

Winn gobbled incessantly, and the birds obligingly made a lot of noise for Roman. Twenty minutes later, Winn heard a lone shot. After the sound waves from the shot had wafted away through the woods, he approached the location of the shot, eager to see Roman's bird.

Doc's estimate of the shot's origin was accurate, for he soon walked straight to a stone-dead gobbler, sprawled between two sycamore trees, in an area swept clean by the bird's flopping. But there was no sign of Roman.

Dr. Winn had been there for two minutes, trying to comprehend the situation, when he heard another shot, 125 yards away to the south. "What's that crazy Roman doing?," he thought. His deliberation was followed by 20 seconds more of silence, then a final, more distant, shot.

He correctly surmised that Roman, after firing, had failed to see a bird fall, and, thinking he had missed, instinctively charged the flock as it escaped. What worried Doc, however, was the ensuing sequence of shots, and the possibility that Roman had accidentally fallen and shot himself.

His anxiety was interrupted when a burly object crashed toward him from the south, through the horseweeds and buck vines. Roman emerged from the thick foliage, having run a circuitous route through the woods, and continued to straggle along a course that would take him past Winn.

Winn yelled as he passed, and Roman, not knowing that he was back to his starting point, stopped and staggered over to him. Dr. Winn pointed to the ground and announced, "Roman, here's your bird."

The disheveled Roman stared, dumbfounded, at the long-bearded gobbler on the ground. After catching his breath, he began to explain what had happened.

After he shot and failed to see a bird fall, he took up

the chase after the flock, thinking that he might have crippled one of them. He said that twice he actually got close enough to one of the gobblers to take shots at him, missing the bird on both occasions.

Winn was almost as astonished as Roman when it became apparent that the second gobbler Roman had been chasing was a virile, unscathed bird. He had just witnessed something he had previously thought to be impossible: a man being able to outrun a healthy, adult gobbler in a footrace.

## JAY

Jay Hines was another of my father's best friends and a frequent visitor to the old OK Hunting Club on Ship Island. Originally from Kentucky, Jay was one of those do-it-all outdoorsmen. Soft-spoken and gentle natured, he loved bass fishing, duck hunting, turkey hunting, and any other type of outdoor pursuit.

In 1960, Dad called up the first bird I ever killed, a jake, but Jay was responsible for calling up my first mature longbeard. The hunt occurred in the spring of 1961. For some reason, Dad was unable to escort me to the woods that morning. Jay and I were hunting The Slash near the Yellow Line Road. As mentioned in Chapter 2, The Slash is a depression that is usually filled with backwater, but it was bone dry that morning.

We approached from the west and heard good gobbling along The Slash before daylight. Jay sat me 20 feet in front of him and slightly to his left, and he began scraping out some basic yelps and clucks on his Lynch box.

The old bird pitched off the roost to our right, into the dry bottom of The Slash. He continued to gobble often and didn't hang up for long, as modern gobblers always seem to do.

The gobbler began to drift very deliberately from right to left, up the bottom of The Slash to us. I was the first to spot him, because I was positioned near the crest of the top bank. When the bird reached us, he turned and began a slow ascent up the bank, headed directly to me.

Jay and I hadn't discussed who was going to do the shooting. Looking back on it, I'm sure he planned for me to shoot all along, because he had placed me in front. The gobbler stepped within range. I was waiting for Jay to shoot, deferring to my elder, as we were trained to do in that era.

I almost waited too long, because when the bird got to 20 steps, he began to get tense, and I heard Jay whisper, "Shoot!" I didn't need to be told more than once, and I busted the old gobbler with one shot from my full-choked Sweet Sixteen Browning.

With only a 16 gauge, I was fortunate that the bird was as close as he was. If I were using a gun that light-weight today, I'd be as nervous as a topless waitress at a dairyman's convention. As Col. Charles Askins would say about using a gun that small on turkeys, "Don't bring a boy to do a man's job."

As it turned out, that bird was, and still is, one of the largest and best gobblers I ever killed. He was well above average for a Mississippi gobbler, a solid 20 pounds, with the spurs longer than any of my later birds: 1-3/8 inches.

That was only my second bird, but it was my first trophy gobbler. Jay was just as excited about the bird as I was. Dad was so impressed with Jay's unselfishness that he resolved to do everything in his power to help Jay get a gobbler for himself that same day.

Dad was never too excited about afternoon turkey hunting. When the gobbling stopped, he usually did the same. And our birds never have been too accommodating about afternoon gobbling. We were scheduled to return home that night, meaning that drastic measures were needed if Jay were to get a bird that afternoon. Those drastic measures took the following shape.

For years Dad had noticed that turkeys would graze in the south end of Bailey's Big Field in the afternoon. That afternoon was no different.

Dad had also noticed that, when tractors worked up to the edge of the woods, the birds would slowly retreat a few yards into the woods, only slightly alarmed. As soon as the tractor turned and headed back to the opposite end of the field again, the turkeys would immediately walk back into the field and resume feeding.

We needed something to imitate a tractor with. Something like a four-wheel-drive vehicle, to facilitate crossing the field. But in 1961, four-wheel-drive vehicles were uncommon at the OK Hunting Club. In those days, the only vehicle available was what we called Sam Wasserman's worst nightmare, a war-surplus Willys Jeep belonging to Dr. Winn.

Sam, the owner of the Tunica Motel, lived adjacent to the motel, and Winn would wake him up at 3:30 every morning before a hunt, revving up his old Jeep for 20 minutes until it was ready to go. On this particular trip, the nightmare was in the repair shop, or otherwise indisposed in the woods somewhere with Dr. Winn. The only imitation tractor available to us was Dad's pink '57 Chevy.

Fortunately the field was dry, and it was decided that the Chevy would be used. Dad put Jay sitting shotgun, with me in the back seat to watch. From a half mile across the field, we began slowly building acceleration until we reached hair-raising speed. My head dimpled the roof of the Chevy with each plowed row we roller-coastered over in the field.

Sure enough, the turkeys performed according to plan, slowly receding into the woods as we approached, indifferent to our break-neck charge. When Dad reached the timbered edge of the field, he swerved the car left, paralleling the woods line, and Jay leaned out as far as he could with his shotgun. When Dad got to the birds' point of entry, he stopped.

It went chalkboard-perfect. As we hoped, the birds had stopped only about 20 steps inside the edge of the woods. Jay calmly picked a caruncled-head with whiskers underneath it and squeezed off one shot. His bird was nearly the trophy that mine was.

We would all later become purists and never entertain again a thought of repeating such heathen tactics. But we were at peace with ourselves on that shining afternoon, because a sportsman had received just compensation for his unselfishness.

A few years later, Jay and Dad were bass fishing in a "blue hole" at Kimble's place over in Arkansas. By chance, Jay had brought along his World War II surplus Colt .45 to plink with. After a couple hours of fishing, a commotion diverted their attention, and they were shocked to see a wild hog trotting along the bank of the blue hole.

Wild hogs were rare along the river at the time, so Jay excitedly grabbed the .45 and unloaded a clip at the beast as it attempted to scramble away. The initial shots pecked the dirt behind the running swine, but Jay was able to adjust and cripple him enough to prevent escape. They quickly paddled over to the bank, and put the beast out of its misery.

They had never known anyone who had killed a wild pig, or anyone who could instruct them on how to dress out the animal. They concluded that, if they were to taste wild pork, the job would be theirs to do.

They knew that one of the hardest tasks facing them was the removal of the hair from the skin. To facilitate what he knew would otherwise be a slavish job, Jay suggested that they take the hog down to the repair shop at the automobile dealership where he worked. There they could separate hair from hide with the steam-cleaner, which was ordinarily used for cleaning car engines. Dad quickly agreed, and the two began their work.

There were no instructions about hog-cleaning on the steam cleaner, so they had to wing it. After several minutes of effort, they noticed a funny smell in the work bay, and discovered that they had effectively parboiled the beast, with most of its hair still intact. I don't recall the details after that, but I know that we never had any wild pork at our house.

One of my saddest moments occurred that night in the fall of 1967 when Dad called me at college to inform me of the sudden death of Jay Hines, at age 49.

Our trips to Tunica County were never quite the same

after that. Dad turkey hunted right up until he passed away in 1994, but his desire to duck hunt and bass fish died along with Jay in 1967. He knew it would never feel right again, without that gentle spirit in the opposite end of the boat.

## Chapter 5

# GEARING UP

The plethora of turkey-hunting gear in the modern sporting-goods stores simply dazzles me. In the 1950s, we had to pick through a store like a bag lady to find turkey-hunting equipment.

In the first place, there were no sporting-goods stores as such, except for one or two in Memphis. The scant amount of gear available in our town could be found only on a small rack in a back corner of the local hardware store.

There you could usually find Lynch box calls, then still being made by old Mr. M. L. Lynch himself. I still have the two old 1950s model Lynch boxes that Dad and I used. They both have been broken and glued, and rebroken and reglued numerous times. I don't know how many times I sat on mine inside a turkey blind.

There were hardly any other commercially-produced calls available to us in the 1950s. The first time I ever saw anyone with a diaphragm mouth call was in the 1968 spring season. Those first diaphragm calls had only one thin rubber reed, and sounded like a cross between a canary and a whistling coffee pot. Nonetheless, we did call up some turkeys with the rudimentary things.

We would readily try any new type of turkey call that we came across. Once, one of Dr. Winn's friends from Nashville came down to Tunica to hunt with us. He promptly displayed an odd-looking turkey call that he said was produced by a call maker from his area. It looked somewhat similar to present-day owl hooters—a cylindrical object with a mouthpiece projecting from its side and a hole just above it on the same side.

He offered the call to anyone who would blow on it, and an egotistical guest of Dad's from Louisiana was the first to volunteer. The would-be calling champion huffed up a big breath and blew into the strange contraption with all his might. Immediately there was an explosion of white smoke in the room, and the dazed performer sheepishly looked up with his face and hair completely covered with talcum powder. The gag call was never taken to the woods.

Camouflage was also practically unavailable in our area then. I started out in war surplus, o.d. green pants, coats, and caps. My hunting boots were plain rubber knee boots or low-cut leather work-boots, and my long johns were old sweat pants. I also remember using a war surplus, wire-frame head net for holding off the fog of mosquitos in our woods.

I also turned up somehow with an old G.I.-issue mosquito bomb. It literally was the shape and size of a small bomb, with a screw-type valve on one end that released a foul-smelling, but effective, mist into the air. I haven't seen another one like it since the early '60s. They probably went the way of many other environmentally-incorrect concoctions that have been banned over the past 30 years.

Now we have turkey-hunting clothing in every conceivable camouflage pattern, calls of every description, and many other related goodies made for the comfort and success of the modern hunter. This profusion of stuff has a double edge to it for the old-time hunter. While finding it much easier to locate gear, the old-timer bemoans the downside to such abundance—that he must share his favorite turkey ridge with a geometrically expanding number of new hunters.

In Mississippi River country, it could be stated at one time that the box call was the king of calls. In the hills of Mississippi and Alabama years ago, the authentic wing-bone caller or a homemade slate was probably the preferred call.

I don't think Gallup has done a poll on the subject, but it seems that more hunters use the diaphragm mouth call now than any other. Newer calls include the push-pin, glass-slate, aluminum-slate, and tube types, and within these general classes are many variations.

I've experimented with almost every type of call in my turkey-hunting career. Maybe it's tradition, but I always seem to wind up using old hinged-lid box calls more than any other type. The box call I started with was one of the types made by gluing several pieces of wood together. Glued-together calls generally seem to have a sweeter, purer tone than most wild turkey hens you hear. If you listen to real hens, you'll probably notice that, although a few make pure-sounding calls, the majority sound somewhat scratchy and raspy.

I noticed for years that only a few hinged-lid box calls had the raspy sound I wanted. The raspier ones were calls carved from solid blocks of very dense wood, such as walnut. The only ones ever available commercially in our area were the old original Tom Turpin boxes and Stribling boxes.

Stribling boxes were relatively rare, found almost exclusively in a small local region centered around Bolivar County, the home county of Mr. Stribling. By the time I decided that I needed a raspier box call, Turpin and Stribling calls were no longer being produced.

John Eddleman and I finally decided that, if we wanted to have raspier box calls, we'd have to make them ourselves. Using a borrowed Stribling box as a pattern, we carved our first calls from solid blocks of walnut that were sawed from a log cut on Whiskey Island in Tunica County.

I stopped after we had made a couple of calls, but Eddleman got hooked and made three dozen or so, becoming quite proficient at it. The calls he made sound better than any I've heard, with the possible exception of some well-aged, original Turpin calls.

I had great success with my new box call the very first season I began using it. In fact, I was able to call up and kill a big gobbler with it the first four hunts I went on, one in Alabama and three in Mississippi. It's an especially satisfying experience to call up a gobbler with a box call made by your own hands from wood grown in your own hunting woods.

I had never lost a turkey call in my life, but on the last day of the spring season two years after we made the first calls, I left my cherished new call in the woods. I didn't miss it until I consolidated my hunting gear on the night before the following fall season. I feverishly tried to remember the last time I had seen it, and I finally realized that it had been the last morning of the previous spring season.

I tried to remember the exact route that I followed on that last spring day. When I went fall hunting, I traced my earlier steps as well as I could, but I failed to locate my prize.

I tried again to find it the next year, and I finally did at the end of the spring season. It was like finding an old friend, but by then the box had been lying in the woods exposed to the elements for an entire year. Luckily, I had coated it with linseed oil, which kept it from completely rotting, but the original density of the wood had diminished somewhat, and it didn't sound the same.

I worked diligently on the box for a couple of years, treating it with epoxy wood-filler and shellacs, to seal and restore the wood and bring back as much of the original tone as possible. Finally, my old dear friend was recovered enough to get off the disabled list and return to the starting rotation, in one of the pockets of my hunting coat.

*Box Calls made by Wade Wineman, Jr. And John Eddleman. L. to r., the prized Stribling-style box call that was left in the woods for a year, a Turpin-style box, and a Stribling-style box made with thicker sides and lid for extra volume.*

## Chapter 6

# LYNCHED BY A HEN

When you enter a sporting goods store the week before the opening of the spring turkey season, what's the thing that impresses you most? In our region, the thing you notice most is the grand cacophony from the rear corner of the store. Sometimes, jake yelps made by a novice caller confuse you and for an instant you could almost swear you'd walked into the dog pound.

When you come to your senses, you might hear other peculiar sounds, too. Low scratching noises, peeps, tweets, and every other sound capable of being produced with rubber, wood, and plastic by the mouth and hand of man. Every year there are more models and brands of turkey calls, and every year the sounds in the back of the store amplify and become more varied.

Don't make your final judgment of a call in the back of a store. The store's acoustics may enhance the sound of some calls and devastate the sound of others. A mouth call may sound exactly like an instructional cassette in the back of the store, but it might sound like a circumcised dachshund in the woods. Conversely, and this is particularly true of box calls, a call frequently sounds better in the woods than in the store.

Before you purchase your next call, try to find an experienced hunter who already has one like it, and field test it with him. Try to conduct your test like this. Walk into the woods at least a hundred yards from the nearest road, field, or clearing. Then tell your friend to walk away from you at least 70 or 80 yards farther and start calling with his call.

Listen carefully, and concentrate on comparing the sound to actual turkey hen sounds as you remember them. Or, if you haven't heard many hens in the wild yet, compare them with recordings you've been listening to.

Many times, the calls that sounded good in the store won't be so hot in the woods, and vice versa. Reserve final approval of a call until after it can pass this simple test.

One of my early experiences illustrates how calls can sound different and play tricks on your ears in the woods.

One morning in the early days of the old OK Club, Dad and I went together down to the north side of Old River Runout on Seabrook's. He had located a massive flock of good gobbling birds strung out along the Old River depression, and our plan was to spread out far enough apart to prevent us from interfering with each other, and approach Old River from the north. We parted, and I walked west a quarter-mile away from Dad before I turned to approach Old River.

There was so much gobbling that morning that I had difficulty deciding which bird to go to. I finally chose the nearest one, set up my blind, and began to yelp and cluck. The birds were soon off the roost, and a dominant gobbler began to work slowly to me from the south.

The gobbler didn't hang up until he was almost in gun range. When he reached that point, he began the characteristic windshield-wiper sweep in front of me, drifting slowly to my left, then back to my right, then retracing the same route.

After 45 minutes of windshield wiping, the gobbler held in the same spot for several minutes, then seemed to move slowly my way. The bird's gobbling was incessant. He had a good "feel" to him. I judged it to be better than 50:50 that I would soon be measuring his spurs.

Before the gobbler moved within range, I began to hear familiar, wooden scraping sounds emanating from 50 yards to the left of me—a Lynch box! I knew that sound well. I had listened to Dad calling on his Lynch innumerable times at point-blank distance in the motel, in the Blue & White, in Seabrook's cabin, and while sitting next to him in the woods. The sounds I was hearing sounded identical to his yelps.

My mind's eye painted a portrait of Dad walking around behind me, trying to call up my bird. His gobbler must have left him, I thought, and for him to be over in my part of the woods, he must have become disoriented. Or, worse, he knew exactly where he was and was selfishly trying to compete with his teenage son. The latter occurrence would have been out of character for him, but gobbling turkeys have been known to cause temporary insanity in individuals.

After a few minutes, the mysterious caller started moving, first to a point directly behind me, then back east again, farther from me than before.

While all of this was occurring, I became aware that my gobbler had gone silent. After a few more minutes the hen calls also ceased, and for the first time that day, I heard no turkey sounds anywhere in the woods.

I waited another hour and a half, thinking that the bird that was once almost at my fingertips would somehow return. I finally gave up in total disgust and defeat, and dragged myself back to the rendezvous point to meet Dad. My own father had called my gobbler off me!

Dad was already there waiting when I got back. He saw the hang-dog look on my face and asked me about my hunt. I couldn't wait to unload on him, and did. I told him about the story-book beginning to my morning, about all the gobbling, about how the dominant bird marched right up to me, about how I was only moments away from busting the old bird in the head, about how I heard him saunter up beside me, calling real loud, and about how he had called my bird right off me.

Few times did I ever hear my father laugh like that, and few times was I ever as mad at him as I was then. When he quit chuckling, he described the events of his morning to me.

"I went in to Old River as we planned, and heard good gobbling. My birds all shut up as soon as they hit the ground and went off to the east with hens.

I got a rounder on them, but didn't hear them gobble anymore and couldn't locate them again. I went east and was at least a half-mile from where you were for the rest of the morning. Son, that gobbler of yours got pulled away by a live hen this morning!"

Since then, I've paid more attention to every hen yelp in the woods, and it's remarkable how many I still hear that sound just like my dad's old Lynch box.

Chapter 7

# THE BIG MOUTH OF BIG BEND

I remember clearly how the gobbler got the moniker of "Big Mouth" put on him. Big Mouth certainly wasn't an original name, but no one could originate one more appropriate for him.

My hunting journal shows that it was in the spring of 1981, a dry spring with low river levels. Big Mouth didn't distinguish himself early in the spring, but later on, he was a real piece of work. My journal also shows that I was the one who first made contact with him.

His haunts were in the northern portion of the "Big Bend" region of Ship Island, so called because Old River makes a great looping bend around the eastern periphery of this contiguous tract of woodland.

In dry years, Big Bend is one prime turkey area. The spring of 1981 was no exception. Turkeys were everywhere and the gobbling was clamorous. The turkey population was at a peak, just before a fowl pox die-off that would strike within a year.

I was introduced to Big Mouth just east of the Log Dump Road, at daylight on April 5. You couldn't dream about weather being more perfect than the weather was that day. My journal shows a temperature range from the high '40s to the mid '60s, with low humidity, fair skies, and calm winds. "Beautiful day.... stars brilliant," it states about the pre-dawn conditions.

The forest canopy was beginning to thicken, but the flat woods floor was still winterlike, and I was unable to safely approach to within 150 steps of the gobbler's roost.

Big Mouth's demeanor early in the season belied his name. On this morning his gobbling was reticent; he gobbled infrequently, and only at barred owls—not at their hoots, but only at the hair-raising screeches they sometimes make in the early morning. He responded neither to me nor to the hens roosting nearby.

The gobbler's disinterest in the hens helped me to decide my strategy. Judging him to be a difficult bird to call, I softly tree-yelped in the opposite direction first. Then I moved 40 steps closer to him, stood in a tangle of vines against a tree, and didn't call again.

At 5:35, I saw him pitch across in front of me from the roost and alight 90 steps away. Four hens immediately joined him. In spite of the hen competition, I waited without calling for the next hour. I wanted to see if my strategy of moving closer without calling would work.

Occasionally you can be positioned within range of a gobbler when he hangs up at what he thinks is a safe distance from where he last heard the hen call. In this case, however, the gobbler didn't move to me, but continued to stand with the hens, in a continuous strut, at 90 steps.

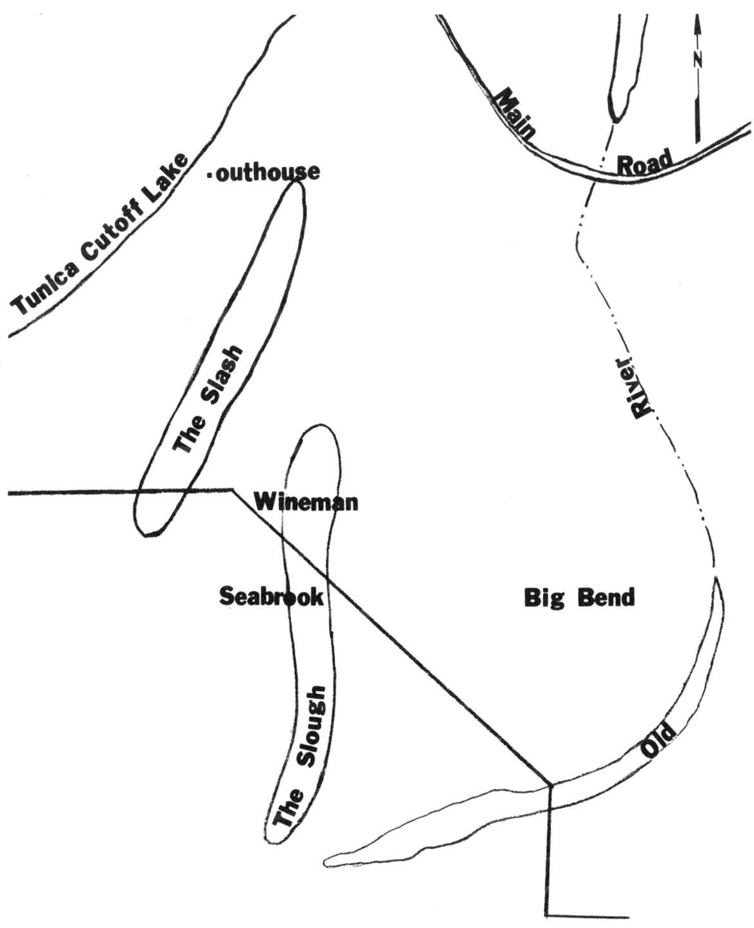


*Map showing the southern portion of Ship Island*

In the first two hours after daylight, I heard seven or eight other distant gobbling birds in every direction. Two were firing-up their gobbling and closing ground slowly, from the north and from the southeast. I could hear hens with both of the approaching birds. They eventually reached Big Mouth at about the same time, and fights began to break out between the flocks. All three flocks charged each other, and the sound of the combatants' thumping breasts and wing-flopping followed soon thereafter, along with the discordant chirping and cackling of the spectators.

According to form, the fights were relatively brief, and when they terminated, all the birds, including Big Mouth, "lit a shuck" and vanished.

I was unable to think of another part of the island that could have more turkeys per acre than the one where I was, so I remained there, calling intermittently. I waited until 11:30, and heard sporadic gobbling from these same three gobblers the whole time, but I never saw nor heard them away from their numerous mistresses.

On several occasions one of the gobblers would bring his convoy slowly my way, only to drift away again. I probably would have stayed in the area all day, except for the fact that I had to depart to pick up some other hunters who wanted to leave the woods early.

I was back on Big Mouth again six days later. The temperature was unseasonably warm, the day windy, overcast, and dewless—not ideal gobbling weather. Big Mouth was the only gobbling bird I heard at daylight, and he was roosted in almost the same area as he was on April 5, with exactly seven hens. I know the exact number; I was able to count them all when I jumped them out of the trees while going to him. After my faux pas, he never gobbled again that day. When he pitched off the roost a little later, he sailed away from me, in the direction the hens had flown.

In the afternoon I returned to the area, but didn't hear

or see anything until 6:09, when he cranked up his gobbling again. I got on him and set up, but it was beginning to get dark and he had roosting on his mind by that time.

He moved slightly toward me, but was still 60 steps away when he flopped up to roost at 6:40, with his harem of hens nearby. I waited until black dark, eased away, and carefully marked the spot for the next morning's action.

My afternoon's effort had enabled me to become privy to the exact location of all the birds. That knowledge allowed me to plot a route to the gobbler away from the hens the next morning and reduce the chances of spooking them.

Under cover of darkness the next day, I was able to get closer to his tree than the hens were—within 80 steps. To be as quiet as possible, I decided not to build a blind and simply stood in a thick, viney place with my gun held at a relaxed version of "parade rest" in front of me. To further minimize movement, I used only a diaphragm call.

A club policy is to assign areas bounded by topographic features to participating hunters, and ask each one to stay within his assigned area, to minimize encroachments. That morning, Dad and I were both hunting in the Big Bend woods, which can easily accommodate two hunters, but has few landmarks or topographic features clearly dividing it. Unbeknownst to me, Dad had somehow set up on the east side of Big Mouth, opposite me.

Big Mouth's hens were not calling much, but luckily for me, the ones that did were 30 steps behind me. I found myself holding the straight flush of turkey hunting—that rare occasion when you find yourself between the big man and his dames, and see your odds jump way up.

Little did I know at the time that all my careful planning would go for nought because of an optical illusion. When the gobbler finally sailed down from his roost, it appeared that he was gliding away from me, and I continued to stand motionless.

I didn't realize soon enough that he was actually headed my way, and, when I did, there wasn't enough time left to shoulder my weapon for the shot he offered when he landed. I could only stand and watch as he touched down in the leaves in a small clearing a mere 25 steps in front of me.

Big Mouth was extraordinarily suspicious after landing. He was as tense as a banjo string, a raw electric wire ready to spark. I dared not raise my gun on a bird that nervous, with the minimal cover available.

One thing I've noticed over the years about turkeys, especially old gobblers, is that the closer they get to you, the more suspicious they become. They get a taut look. You get the feeling they have a sixth sense, like they *know* you're there, even when you make no movement or sound.

Big Mouth, however, was even more suspicious than a typical old gobbler. Sensing that I was there, he slowly started quartering away from me. There was only one object in the entire clearing, a two-inch diameter sapling, really too small to be able to raise a gun without being seen when he passed behind it.

It presented my only opportunity, however, and I decided that I would try to get into warp drive and outdraw him as the sapling briefly obscured his vision.

When Big Mouth passed behind the small tree, I made my move but couldn't match his quickness. He was beyond 3-inch magnum range before I could take a single shot. My hunting journal states, "It was amazing how fast he got away." Even though that was 15 years ago, I still remember his being the swiftest movements by a turkey that I have ever seen.

Each time we gather after a day's hunt, we all sit around and trade tales of the day. When it came Dad's turn that day, his initial remarks were that he'd seen a gobbler do something he had never witnessed before, something completely illogical. He had been working a gobbler on the roost, and the crazy bird pitched down, then almost immediately leaped back up again from the same spot and flew off. It was at least a week later before I told him why his gobbler had flown off like that.

I played with Big Mouth one other time, and saw him hit the ground with his hens, ignore my calling, and leave me. Another hunter also tried him, and then we gave him away to somebody else.

Walter Roman wound up with him. Roman has always complained that I tend to put him on gobblers that have been "fooled with" all season. That hasn't always been the case, but I do recollect that Big Mouth was the first of about three gobblers in a row that were handed down to him in a four- or five-year period.

As I recall it, Roman was actually the one who hung the name of Big Mouth on the bird. I put Roman on him on April 21, and, despite having been hunted all season, Big Mouth put on the show of a lifetime for him, gobbling almost continuously from 5:05 to 8:00.

Toward the end of the morning, Roman saw Big Mouth rush into a small clearing within range of his blind. Before Roman could react, the gobbler pounced on a squatting hen, and treaded and serviced her in full view of Roman's disbelieving eyes.

Being the sport he was, Roman didn't shoot Big Mouth while he mated the hen. He didn't want to run the risk of crippling her also, so he decided to wait compassionately until the intimate act was concluded.

Roman paid for his compassion, however. When Big Mouth finished, he instantly darted into a thicket beside the clearing, abandoned the entire area, and wasn't seen or heard from again that day.

No one was able to kill Big Mouth that year. He probably was never harmed by man and died from natural causes, but I'll never know for certain. It's hard for us to recognize birds from year to year on the island by their tendency to frequent the same territories.

You can often do this in the hills, but our flat-swamp birds are affected too much by fluctuating water levels each year. For whatever reason, we didn't have a bird similar to Big Mouth in Big Bend the next year, and we haven't had many as cagey as he was anywhere on the entire island during the last 35 years.

## Chapter 8

# GOING IN CIRCLES

In the spring of 1985, we were in the grip of the worst turkey depression on the island since 1971, a shortage caused not by our archenemy, fowlpox, but by losing consecutive hatches to unusually high river levels in late spring in both 1983 and 1984.

Gobbling, of course, was relatively infrequent that spring, and you counted yourself fortunate when you heard even one on the roost. In spite of the turkey shortage, I had one of my most unforgettable hunts on a beautiful day in the middle of the season. The dawn of that day was christened with heavy dew, something that serious turkey hunters have appreciated since the Alabama Game & Fish Department concluded after a field study many years ago that gobbling activity closely parallels the heaviness of the dew.

Calm winds and fair skies added to my confidence that morning, and warm temperatures, while not particularly important for gobbling, made things more convenient for me, because I could travel in the woods in lighter gloves and clothes.

We're seldom blessed with more than two or three days like that each spring, and whenever we are, it's so inspiring that I find myself thanking God for the experience.

Despite published reports to the contrary, many folks still herald warm weather as a sign of better gobbling. I have hunted on many cold mornings in 37 years, and have satisfied myself that cold weather should be completely disregarded as a deterrent to both total gobbling quantity and the frequency of gobbling by individual gobblers. One of the best mornings I remember occurred when the low for the day was 32 degrees, a record for the date.

I was hunting in Bailey's Woods, at the Boy Scout Field, so named because a local scoutmaster took his troops there for summer campouts many years ago. From the edge of the field, I heard six birds gobble over the backwater at first light: two to the northeast, two to the north, and two to the southeast.

I moved to the northeast corner of the two-acre field and set up just inside the woods on its edge. The two gobblers to the northeast sailed down at daylight and rapidly walked past me just out of range through the weedy field, heading toward two hens south of me.

I was able to shift to the south and call to them after they passed. They didn't gobble much, but they picked up the two hens and returned to a point inside the tree line on the north edge of the field and hung up there, 60 yards from me.

One of the longbeards fanned out in front of his hen and stayed in a strut for a full 30 minutes without folding a feather. The other gobbler treaded and topped his hen, then he and the hen performed a ritual that I have only seen one other time. While the other gobbler strutted, the second

*The author with a nice Ship Island gobbler*

gobbler and his hen ran around in a circle 10 feet in diameter, for the entire 30 minutes. That was the only occasion when I saw a gobbler and a hen do that. On one other occasion, I witnessed a similar ritual involving two jakes, and were it not for that, I would be inclined to believe that it is some type of mating ritual.

I waited until the gobbler and hen stopped chasing

each other before calling again. There was no response, but the strutting gobbler started stepping slowly in my direction, fanned out. He moved straight to a downed treetop that was in range in front of me, then began sliding along it, obscured from my view. I had two brief chances to shoot through holes in the top as he moved along it, but I refrained from bringing my weapon up for fear that the other witnesses would putt at the movement. My decision proved to be a wise one. When the gobbler reached the end of the top, he stepped behind a tree, offering me an excellent opportunity to raise my gun. When he stepped out, he was strutting again. I started to putt, to make him extend his neck, but I hesitated when I saw him turn and head directly to me.

He stayed in a full strut until he was 21 steps from me. I was about to putt when he shortened up into a half strut and sent his cobra neck high into the air to survey for the hen. I squeezed my shot off as soon as the neck went up, and the three-year-old bird was mine.

It was a satisfying conclusion to what had been both an education in wild turkey biology and an exciting hunt. Each time I have an experience like that one, where I'm able to view turkeys for an extended period of time, I learn something new about their behavior: I mean it sincerely when I say that it's far more meaningful to me to be able to witness the small, secret quirks of turkey behavior, and hear their sounds, than it is to reduce one to a stiff, ruffled clump in the leaves.

Of course, there is one exception. The later I go in the season without picking up a dead bird, the more meaningful the latter deed becomes.

## Chapter 9

# THE HANT OF PAW PAW RIDGE

Wild gobblers can sometimes appear to be wills-o'-the-wisp. Specters. Ghosts. Apparitions. Or, in Old-South vernacular, "hants."

You may work a hant for days, or even weeks, but seldom do you even get a glimpse of him. He usually gobbles his head off, but the more you hunt him, the more you tend to doubt that what you're hearing is really a turkey. He can really get to you and play tricks with your mind after a while.

I've attempted to call up hants like this numerous times over the years. I found the most mysterious hant I ever encountered in the spring of 1985. My hunting journal reminds me that I was the first hunter to meet him that spring.

After I had finished setting up a blind, at 4:45 one

afternoon early in the season on "Paw Paw Ridge," I heard a hen yelp. I called sporadically without hearing anything else until 6:05, when my gaze briefly fell on The Hant.

Paw Paw Ridge is one of the thickest ridges on the island, and my field of vision was limited to narrow lanes between the paw-paws and cane. He first appeared when he stepped into one of the lanes, 80 steps from me. He paused briefly and stood tall, as if to ensure that I saw him, then he vanished into the dense understory.

My glimpse of him was as fleeting as a mist in a storm, but it was enough for me to see that he was the size of an ostrich. After he faded into the lushness he paused, because I heard him gobble four times between then and dark. Two of the gobbles were in response to pileated-woodpecker cackles. He answered my calls only once. I failed to hear him fly up to roost at dusk, but decided to return anyway the next morning.

It was drizzling before dawn the next day, but it stopped just as the awakening sun started to brighten the sky. Not surprisingly, The Hant was silent on the roost. I speculated that he was roosted over a flooded area on the east side of the ridge, and I set up facing that direction, at the spot where I had seen him cross the lane the afternoon before.

He didn't answer while he was on the roost, but soon after fly-down time, I heard a lone gobble behind me to the west. He had roosted over Frederick Bayou, a bayou which runs along the west side of Paw Paw Ridge. I had seen him heading east the afternoon before, but he had apparently looped back later to the west side of the ridge without my spotting him.

I shifted quickly to face him. I would never have

selected the spot where I was for a west-facing setup. He was 90 yards from me, and the woods in that direction were much too dense out to 50 yards.

I called him with yelps only, and he closed ground to about 60 to 70 yards, gobbling five times. He didn't stay on course long, however. The next time I heard him, he was 100 steps farther west. I tried to get a rounder on him, but he only gobbled one more time, and I didn't do any more good with him that day.

I hunted Paw Paw Ridge two more times without locating him, once on the afternoon of April 13 and once on the morning of April 14, when I left the woods by 7 a.m. because of rain.

The next time I hunted the ridge was on the morning of April 18. The Hant didn't gobble there, but I heard him to the west, across Frederick Bayou.

Deep water prevented me from wading the bayou, so I hurried back to my Bronco. I raced north in it to the road crossing over the bayou, then around to the west side. I reached The Hant's area, set up, and was barely able to call for the first time before he came off the roost.

He was roosted near the west side of the bayou on the east edge of the Boy Scout Field, so I set up near the west edge of the two-acre field. The only calls he answered on the roost were cackles. When he pitched down, he moved rapidly to a point to my right rear. I couldn't see him, but I heard a wing flop when another bird, presumably a hen, sailed down to meet him.

He stayed south of me for an hour, gobbling two to three times a minute. He wasn't answering me, but he gobbled at every owl call and pileated woodpecker cackle, and also at the propane cannons that were set up to scare cormorants away on the catfish-farm ponds across the levee.

The way that he answered the cannons was strange. The initial boom of the guns was immediately followed by a higher-pitched echo, something like "boom .... *pow,* boom .... *pow.*" The gobbler only answered the echoing *pows,* not the booms.

After an hour, his almost-continuous gobbling ceased for a few minutes. During the respite, he moved around me to the north side of the small field, then started gobbling again, and continued to do so without ceasing for two hours more. Once during that time, he moved to within 60 steps of me, then drifted away again. His gobbling began to diminish after 9, and he went totally silent at 10. At 11, I moved west 100 yards to the road paralleling the field, and started moving north on it, cackling every 100 steps or so. After my third cackle, he gobbled, only 80 steps off the road east of me and north of where the field ended.

I immediately fell to the ground and crawled off the road into the edge of the woods, and waited on him. He adopted the same pattern he had exhibited earlier—slowly working up to 60 steps, gobbling occasionally, then going silent and walking off again. I finally left him for good at 1 p.m.

The Hant was a classic. He gobbled well over 100 times that day. I had worked him with tree yelps and cackles on the roost, and used soft yelping, whines, cackles, and jake gobbles when he was on the ground. He had only answered me when I cackled to him early, before he came off the roost. Hunting a gobbler like him is a captivating, but frustrating experience.

The turkey population was low, and there were few gobbling birds to hunt in 1985. Gobbling in our area typically starts tapering off, even in well-populated years, after the middle of April.

By April 19 of that year, The Hant was the only bird that was still gobbling on Ship Island, and I had concluded that he was a gobbler worth spending the rest of the year on. I had become caught up in an old-fashioned grudge match.

It reminded me of a story my old friend and hunting companion, Willie Clyde Green, had told me about his uncle, Gene Nunnery, the legendary turkey hunter and author of *The Old Pro Turkey Hunter*. He told me about the year that "Mr. Gene" was bewildered by a crafty old gobbler, and spent the entire spring trying to outwit the bird.

There were recapitulations of each day's hunt by all the young hunters who held Mr. Gene in awe around Meridian, Mississippi. Mr. Gene normally killed five or six gobblers each spring, but he never did kill that one, to the amazement of his young admirers.

Of course, the next day I returned to the Boy Scout Field area. I heard The Hant gobble 300 yards east of me, and I went to him. The area west of Frederick Bayou is split by an unnamed depression. To the north of this shallow, wide depression, and between it and the south end of Bailey's 150-acre "Big Field," is a high little ridge shaped like a piece of pie or a triangle, known as "Pie Ridge."

As I approached the bird, I could see that he was roosted directly over Frederick Bayou out from the tip of Pie Ridge, at the confluence of the bayou and the other depression. The backwater had dropped a foot and a half

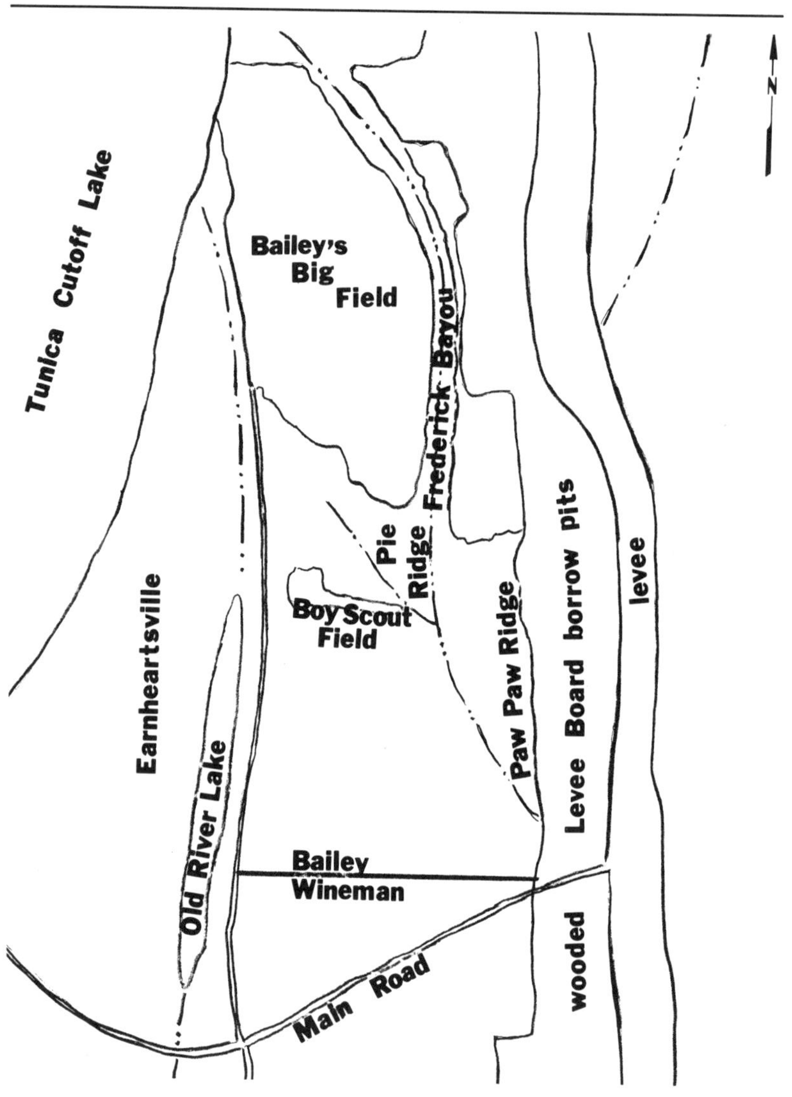


*Map showing the northern portion of Ship Island*

since the preceding day, making the bayou shallow enough for me to wade across and set up on the Paw Paw Ridge.

Knowing how difficult the bird would be to lure, I

changed strategies. I decided to call to The Hant first, then using the natural thickness of Paw Paw Ridge, move 60 steps closer and refrain from calling again. If he hung up in relation to the calls he heard, he might be within shotgun range of where I actually stood. I tree-clucked and cackled twice. He answered and I moved up, as planned, to within shooting range of the water in Frederick Bayou. When I reached that point, I was only 80 yards from The Hant's tree, which was south of me, down the bayou.

He gobbled 50 or 60 times on the roost, and didn't come down until 6:48, an hour and 15 minutes later than normal. Before he pitched down, I began to hear hens on the ground to my right rear. They were moving my way, purring and occasionally yelping. It sounded like the hens were on my side of the bayou, which, if true, meant that I was fortuitously positioned between The Hant and his harem.

I was soon disappointed, however. I heard one of the hens flop her wings twice, and I realized they were near enough for me to see them. I slowly turned my head, and my hopes were dashed when I saw them across the water from me on Pie Ridge.

A moment later, The Hant pitched off his roost, sailed straight down the center of Frederick Bayou until he was opposite the hens, then veered left and alighted on Pie Ridge.

I actually could have wing-shot him as he sailed down the bayou. In my youth I wouldn't have hesitated on such an occasion, but over the years I've gradually become a purist about wild turkeys. Besides, with 12 days left in the season, I was confident that I would have other chances at him.

Had I known the hens were on the ridge across the water from me that morning, I would have called more often. I've found that calling frequency should generally increase as competition from other hens calling increases. It wasn't calling, however, that foiled me that time. It was positioning. Obviously, the better alternative always is to be on the same side of the water with your birds.

At midday I moved around to Pie Ridge and set up there. I stayed for the rest of the afternoon, calling every 20 minutes or so. I hoped that The Hant would return, to fly up to roost again from the end of Pie Ridge, but at dark there had been no sign of him. He had apparently changed his travel pattern and his roost tree.

The next morning I heard him gobble 200 yards south down Frederick Bayou from the previous day's roost, where the bayou and the depression joined. Knowing that he must have flown to roost from the west side of the bayou the afternoon before, and assuming he would fly back down there, I set up on the west side 100 steps from him.

It was thick enough there to facilitate movement calling, so I was able to back away from my intended set-up place, move parallel to him, and call from three different locations (to simulate a hen walking around) before silently returning to my setup spot.

The Hant gobbled wildly on the roost again, but came down late, at 6:24. As usual, he was disdainful of my calling and did the unexpected. He flew down, not on the west side from where he went up, but on the east side, on Paw Paw Ridge, exactly where I'd been set up the day before!

The river was down another foot and a half, and I was forced again to wade across Frederick Bayou again to get to him. He was moving north, up the ridge, gobbling more often on the ground than on previous days, and it was easier for me to get a rounder on him and keep him located.

Unlike when he was on the roost, he answered almost every call on the ground, but I noticed that he was continually moving away from me, up the ridge. I got another rounder north of him, but by the time I set up, he had cycled into a silent mode and refused to gobble at anything.

With my patience and my purity both spent, I finally decided to stalk the danged bird on the thick ridge. I knew he was still somewhere south of me, so I began creeping down the ridge in that direction. After only a few minutes, I glimpsed him and the hens, and I immediately halted, in a standing position, in deep shade.

Amazingly, I had gone unnoticed by all of the birds, and The Hant was grazing very slowly in my direction. After a few steps, he froze and stared straight at me for a full 30 minutes—an incredible period of time for a turkey (and a hunter) to stand motionless. He was only 45 to 50 steps away, and I thought about trying him at that range, but decided against it.

When he finally started moving and went out of sight behind a tangle of foliage, I sank cautiously to the ground and crawled to a tree closer to him, from where I expected to have a shot. A minute or less transpired while I did this, but when I reached the tree and peeped from behind it, he and his hens had vanished.

I returned to the island a few days later to hunt alone, one day before Dad and Walter Roman came up for the final two days of the season. Since The Hant was the only gobbling bird left, I knew they would want to hunt him and that my youth would defer to their age.

In a final attempt to locate another longbeard, I scouted other areas thoroughly, but was unable to find any more sign or gobbling activity. When the three of us planned strategy the night before the hunt, I offered The Hant to Roman. The only thing I told him was that I knew where a good gobbling turkey was and that I'd put him on the bird.

Dad and I dropped Roman off at the north end of Bailey's woods before daylight the next day. I knew that Dad and I would both strike out, and that's exactly what we did. Roman and Dad both liked to come out of the woods as soon as the gobbling ceased, or at 9 a.m., whichever came earlier. I usually hunted at least until noon, but I terminated my hunt early that day, anxious to hear Roman's narrative about The Hant.

According to form, Roman was there waiting for me at the north end of the woods when I arrived to pick him up. I could tell he was fired-up as he recounted the events of the morning.

He had gone to a gobbler that was gobbling his waddles off, and at daylight the bird sailed off the roost to hens on the ground. The birds gradually worked their way around him and went into Bailey's Big Field.

He was able to crawl to the edge of the field and watch the gobbler and the hens with his binoculars. The old fellow gobbled without stopping from 5:15 to 8:15 a.m., but none of the birds would come to him.

When Roman had finished his narrative, I casually mentioned to him that his experience was remarkably similar to mine. With that, he nodded, and with a sarcastic chuckle pronounced, "Well, that explains it, you've been harassing the bird all season, haven't you?"

I told him, "No, I haven't hunted him the whole season, but in the last 16 days I've hunted him seven times." Roman just laughed and said, "Is that any way to treat your guests?"

I answered, "Well, which would you like better, to hear an uncallable bird gobble 100 times in a morning, or walk around in a section of woods that's as quiet as a tomb, and count mulberry trees and indigo buntings?"

Roman acknowledged my reasoning with a nod, but even now, 11 years later, he still reminds me about the tendency he says I have to put guests on frazzled, leftover gobblers.

Despite his complaining, Roman didn't volunteer to give the bird back to one of us and scout a different section of the island the next morning. That night, while gulping down onion rings before our catfish was served at the cafe, Roman was ambivalent about how he should work the ornery bird the next day.

I suggested to him and Dad that we surround The Hant while he was still on the roost, and call to him from three sides; it was a strategy I had used only one other time. Roman quickly agreed to the plan. For him, one session with The Hant had been sufficient to conclude that a single man was incapable of bringing him off the island.

The only other time I had done such a thing was when I was in college, on a hunt with a friend at Noxubee Refuge, in east Mississippi, where gobblers were scarcer than hunters. My friend and I heard a single bird gobble one morning, and we decided to position ourselves on opposite sides of the roost tree.

As is often typical on public areas, ours were not the only ears that heard the lone bird's gobbles. When I got into position, I not only recognized my friend's calling on the other side of the tree, but also began to hear two other callers who were positioned 90 degrees to my left and right. We literally had the gobbler surrounded on all four sides.

These days, it's a common occurrence to hear about a caller gobbling to a bird. I do it often myself, if the circumstances are right. But in the 1960s, gobbling, like four-letter words on t.v. shows, was still considered to be risque. You would hear about people gobbling occasionally, but it kind of took your breath when you did. Hunters who gobbled were considered to be about half-a-bubble off plumb.

Nonetheless, I had never faced the kind of competition I faced that morning. At the risk of being shunned from society, I started gobbling my tail off with my box call, while my three competitors simply yelped and clucked.

The four of us effectively neutralized each other. Predictably, after a few minutes of the unharmonized calling, the gobbler selected the only reasonable alternative presented to him. Like a helicopter, he lifted straight up, to maximum gobbler altitude, and flew away, high over us all, into the hinterlands of the refuge.

Back in town later, after the word hit the street, I heard snickering, and a couple of people even asked me flat out, "Buddy said you were gobbling to a bird on the roost yesterday. Don't you know how you're supposed to call turkeys?"

Roman, Dad, and I were greeted with a cloudy and

humid predawn on the last day of the season, our last chance at The Hant. Thankfully, though, the winds were calm.

Assuming that the bull-headed gobbler would be roosted over Frederick Bayou, we had crafted a plan of attack. It was agreed that Dad would approach the roost tree from the Boy Scout Field, west of the bayou. Roman would approach from the north, on Pie Ridge, and I would position myself on the east side of Frederick Bayou, on Paw Paw Ridge.

We heard The Hant gobbling well before first light. Our assumption was correct about his roost location. He was over the bayou just north of the confluence of the bayou and the depression. Because of the forest's late-season lushness, we were all able to move in near his roost tree without his detecting any of us.

Roman had pointed out a hen nest with 11 eggs in it to me the day before, which indicated to me that the hens would soon be deserting the gobblers for full-time matriarchal duties. That was confirmed by the fact that there seemed to be no hens roosted near The Hant.

Dad was set up only 100 steps from the bird, at the east end of the Boy Scout Field. Roman and I were even closer. After setting up, I only made soft tree clucks and yelps, and The Hant answered them well. I could easily hear Dad and Roman begin to call also.

After calling a few times, I started moving toward the gobbler, utilizing the exceptional thickness on Paw Paw Ridge. I reached the edge of a shelf of land that sloped gradually down to the bayou, 40 steps away. From that vantage point, I was only 70 steps from his roost on the far side of the bayou. I stopped there, well hidden in a thicket of vines and cane.

At 5:31, the old boy simply hopped from his limb and dropped directly to the ground beneath his tree. I saw him clearly. If I'd been set up slightly closer to the bayou, I could have shot him as he alighted on the other side.

He hit the ground walking, and quickly moved southwest, directly toward Dad. The rapidly-falling river had retreated from the shallow depression on the west side of Pie Ridge, and The Hant crossed it, gobbling every other step.

As the gobbler was approaching Dad, he veered and passed by his blind barely out of gun range. Then he marched to a point 125 yards south of Dad, stopped, and began gobbling impudently back at him.

A light drizzle began, and I could hear that Dad was continuing to work the bird. I went back to join Roman at the Bronco, and listen for the shot that probably wouldn't occur.

Dad worked the gobbler until the rain intensified to a downpour and the bird stopped gobbling. When he returned to the Bronco, he offered to give The Hant back to Roman or me, but with prospects of bad weather for the remainder of the day, we both decided to call it a season.

I found myself after the season worrying about the possibility that The Hant had passed-on his genes. I hope that he was sterile, and I hope they never find any of his DNA preserved in the body of a mummified mosquito. We don't need any more like him on Ship Island.

## Chapter 10

# THE PARTY LINE

Ship Island was blessed with a bountiful population of wild turkeys in the spring of 1977. Its bronzed residents had come a long way from the great fowlpox die-off of 1971.

The river also behaved the entire spring, remaining low enough to permit access to the island with four-wheel-drive vehicles instead of boats. Each time I thumb through my hunting journal and reach the scribbled heading, "Spring, 1977," a tale of a novice hunter flits before my mind's eye and evokes fond memories.

The journal reports the date as April 24, 1977, the date that year of "springing forward" from standard to daylight saving time. The temperature range for the day was 57 to 64 degrees, a fairly chilly day for that late in the spring, and skies were overcast and winds light. Normally we don't expect to have exceptional gobbling under such conditions, but things ran counter to expectations that morning.

One of Dad's hill friends, Bob Johnson, was over to hunt with us. Dad and Bob had been good friends for many years on both professional and social levels, but Bob had come to Tunica to hunt with us only one other time. It had been just a year earlier, and that occasion had been his maiden voyage into the sport of turkey hunting.

Bob, a likable and upbeat sort, was always poking fun at my father, laughing and making light of everything. Bob had come as a novice to Ship Island in 1976, and as one of us always does when we have a new initiate, Dad escorted him and called for him.

Dad had been able to call up one of those rare birds, a gobbler that works fast and easy into close range, and Bob had dispatched it pronto. He, of course, made great fun of the sport, declaring how disappointed he was to find that supposedly hard-to-kill turkey gobblers were actually easier to kill than the quail and doves he hunted in the hills. Bob continued to carry on with this demeaning line of chatter, in spite of Dad's reminding him that his guide had done almost all of the work necessary to lure the bird into shotgun range.

Long-standing Ship Island policy is that guests will be guided by a host on their first trip only. On subsequent trips they are shoved out of the nest and into the woods on their own. A guest is always instructed on his first hunt to carefully observe every move and calling technique of the guiding host, so that he will attain self-sufficiency as quickly as possible.

It was quite clear that Dad had lamented the fact that Bob's first hunt had been so quick, easy, and successful. During the following year he eagerly anticipated Johnson's return, and the certain humiliation that he would receive when he hunted solo for one of the whiskered old men of the woods.

Bob came to camp the night before his second hunt, the next spring. After we had finished our steak supper, Dad insisted that Bob have a lesson on how to call. As usual, Bob snickered and guffawed and made fun of Dad's solemnity, remarking that he didn't need further instruction; that the brief experience he had the previous year was enough to kill something as moronic as a wild turkey.

Bob finally relented to the nagging, and Dad managed to spoon-feed him a few series of basic five- and six-note yelps, with a cluck or two occasionally mixed in for variety.

It was like Christmas Eve to Dad when he got into bed that night. He had trouble dozing off, what with all the blissful thoughts of a certain come-uppance in store for the supercilious Johnson the next morning.

Dad and another guest planned to hunt in Big Bend that morning, and it fell to me to drop Bob off along the Roman Road. It was still 30 minutes before first light when we arrived at the drop point. I needed the additional time to reach my spot at the south line before day broke.

I told Bob that turkeys would probably be roosted over The Slash west of him, and he should move that way before daylight and listen for gobbling. I left him standing in the gloomy blackness in the middle of the road, and headed off to The Slough area at the south line.

I managed to have a delightful hunt that morning. I was able to work a big gobbler and a group of hens off the roost, and was later entertained for 30 minutes by constant gobbling and a fight before killing an 18-pound participator.

Thirty minutes after I shot, I was carrying my gobbler back to the Bronco and clearly heard a single shot less than a mile north of me in the Roman Road area. My initial reaction when I heard it was that it couldn't possibly have been Bob Johnson's shot. The average tenderfoot needs two or three years to learn terrain and turkey-habits well enough to kill a gobbler by himself, and certainly so if he is to kill one so quickly after fly-down time. And, Bob was no average tenderfoot; he was a cocky tenderfoot.

After depositing my bird at the Bronco, I scouted the south line area for a couple of hours more before returning to the Roman Road to wait for Johnson to come out of the woods. When I reached the rendezvous point, I was stunned to find him lying asleep at the edge of the road with a huge, stiff longbeard stretched out beside him.

He sleepily recounted his story to me. "When you dropped me off, it was totally black, and I was a little nervous about getting lost, especially since it was my first time to be alone on the island. I decided not to move to the Slash like you told me. As a matter of fact, I never moved all morning. I just stayed here on the road where you dropped me. I didn't hear any gobbling before daylight, so I just waited until the sky brightened, pulled out that box call your Dad loaned me, and made two longs and a short. I heard a loud gobble, pretty close to the road, and I waited a couple more minutes and made two longs and a short again. Right away I heard another gobble, closer than the first one. I didn't know what to do next, so I waited a while, then made two longs and a short another time. There was another gobble, real close. About five minutes after that I saw a giant, fluorescent-white head snaking through the weeds in front of me, so I raised my shotgun and pulled the trigger. This gobbler here was so close to me, he almost fell in the road. I never left the road the whole morning."

Well, when we got back to camp you should have seen Dad. I never saw a mouth open wider or a pair of shoulders slumped lower than his were when he saw the two big gobblers and learned that only one was mine. He hated to ask Bob to tell his story, but to refuse would have been contrary to camp custom. With a baboon grin on his face, Bob sat down and began. The story that he recounted to Dad was much more embellished than the one he'd reported to me earlier, and you could tell that Dad was seething inside as it dragged on and on.

When Bob had finished, I asked him to slowly repeat the part about the calls he had made to the gobbler. I wanted to make sure that Dad had the pleasure of seeing how well his instruction had been absorbed by Bob the night before, and I also wanted Dad to hear again Bob's descriptions of the calls he had used. After I asked him, Bob replied, "Yeah, Wade, the only call I ever made was two longs and a short."

Dad replied, "Two longs and a short? What do you mean by that—two yelps and a cluck?"

Bob answered, "If that's what they're called, I guess so, but to me, they were just two longs and a short."

Dad just had to ask the question, and did, "Bob, why did you make only two yelps every time? Don't you know that a turkey hunter seldom makes just two yelps? Real-live hens usually make more, and they mix it up some. And, besides, that's not the way I taught you, anyhow. I always made five or six yelps when I was teaching you last night."

Bob was gazing up at Dad from his chair, and his countenance changed from cheerful to sober as he explained, "I know you did, Wade, but I decided that would be the best combination for me to use. You see, when I was in high school in Desoto County, I had a girl-friend who lived way out in the country. Her family couldn't afford a private phone line, so they were on the party line. And, the way her phone rang on the party line was...two longs and a short."

## Chapter 11

# Up Periscope!

Whereas in the Great Depression, Americans spent almost every waking moment trying to earn an extra nickel for a loaf of bread, we have now, for the most part, become a nation of hedonists.

This, of course, is the result of the progression (or regression, in the eyes of some) from a six-day to a five-day work week, or even to a four-day work week for a few, and the resulting increase in time available for leisure activities. Now, many of our hunting camps are literally over-run with hunters on weekends, especially on opening weekend.

Each hunting camp seems to have its own personality. At some camps the standard operating procedure is sour mash and poker after supper. At others, the evening routine might include activities such as recollections by the fireplace of legendary gobblers from the camp's turkey gobbler Hall of Fame.

During our camp's first 20 years, the former activity prevailed, but with age comes wisdom, and now the latter suits us just fine.

Our Hall of Fame is a large one. It's large because most of the turkeys nominated over the years were ones that were never killed, and it seems like we've always had more in that category than in the other one. Since their nomination into the Hall many years ago, and with annual recountings of the qualifying tales, several of the Hall's members have acquired legendary, almost mythical status.

Occasionally at our post-repast, fireside-Hall-of-Fame discussions, reminiscences also arise about gobblers that failed to accomplish an escape and were "reduced to possession." At Hall-of-Fame meetings when my father was alive, it seemed he would always recycle his account of a memorable hunt involving one of these cagey, but unlucky, gobblers.

The hunt occurred during the old OK Club days, pre-1968, and the setting was in the Old River Runout country down on Seabrook. Dad had unsuccessfully devoted the majority of his spring season to working an old gobbler that had managed to stay otherwise occupied squiring an enormous bordello of hens.

Time was expiring for the spring season, and Dad had already given up on the old bird until he began to notice signs that most of the hens in the woods were beginning to leave the gobblers. Time and again he observed hens that would hold like quail, then explode at the last minute from the sides of roads as he walked by. He knew these behavioral aberrations were indications that the hens were guarding nests.

Thinking that his odds of luring the obstinate old longbeard were improving, Dad renewed his assault on him. On the last weekend of the season, he drove his Bronco down to the runout area for one last hunt. He parked under the same old mulberry tree that leaned out over the trail almost like a weeping willow. He had learned on his earlier hunts that the mulberry was located at just the right place from which he could enter the gobbler's section of woods and approach him.

Dad waited under the tree until the deep blackness started gathering a tinge of gray and the first cardinal tweets began. The barred owl hoots were still too infrequent to assist him in zeroing in on the gobbler's roost tree, so he cupped his hands around his mouth and produced the morning's first artificial hoot in that section of woods.

The gobbler didn't disappoint him. As if he were waiting for the first owl, the bird responded almost simultaneously and caused Dad to choke on his hoot and prematurely terminate it. The gobble was the first of a sequence, and the bird's rate of gobbling gradually escalated from once per minute to three or four times a minute.

That morning seemed scripted to be one of those rare ones when everything goes right. None of his calls squawked in his pocket. Dad was unusually successful at weaving his way around the small limbs on the forest floor that would potentially snap under the weight of his foot as he slipped toward the gobbler's tree. And no hens spooked off their roosts and flew away putting loudly as he approached the bronze brute.

He found a tree wider than his shoulders at just the right distance from the gobbler's roost. And the tree was almost due east of the roost, so he would be facing away from the sun when he looked at the bird. And incredibly, the tree had neither a spine-distorting buck vine attached to its side, nor a butt-aching root at its base.

Dad put up his military camo net blind and blew up his riding-mower innertube. Then he sat down comfortably and went into his calling routine.

Soon the assertive bird was gobbling at the hoot of every owl, the cackle of every pileated, and every hen call that Dad made.

Preposterously, the bird even gobbled once at a distant towboat horn, five miles away on the river, and once also at the sound of a paddle thumping the gunwale of a johnboat on Old River Lake.

The gobbler was doing everything chalkboard-perfect. He hopped off the roost right on time. The bird must have known that the number of hens in the area near his tree was minimal, because he didn't even stop to strut after alighting. He immediately moved north, slinking slowly, but continuously, toward Dad.

Dad could occasionally sight the bird's obscure movement through the yellow-tops and poison-ivy stems, which stood tall in the lateness of spring. Each time the movements paused, a cobra of a head, radiating fluorescent whiteness in the muted grayness of early dawn, slowly rose above the weeds to scout for the beckoning hen.

After straining to focus on the spot where he last saw movement, Dad realized that the gobbler had disappeared. His eyes swept slowly left and right. No bird. He waited a full 20 minutes, his eyes panning over the same scene innumerable times. He concluded that the gobbler had departed, probably meandering over to commandeer a real hen he had seen at a distance through the woods.

*Wade, Sr. bags another*

This had happened to him a thousand times. "Still amazing," he thought, "how a full-grown gobbler can slink along, low to the ground, almost as low as a snake sometimes, and, after stopping, extend just enough of his head above the weeds to investigate."

Dad considered calling with his box call again, but until he saw the bird, or heard him gobble again, he couldn't risk moving. The bird might be focusing on him while hunkering in the yellowtops. He waited... and waited... 10 more minutes... then another 15.

The bird suddenly stepped out from behind the yellowtops, and began walking at a deliberate pace, straight toward Dad. Between them was a small, open clearing that offered no cover for the bird to step behind, cover that would screen from the gobbler's eyes the movement when Dad raised his gun. Dad was forced to simply wait as the tall gobbler continued to advance.

A 28-inch diameter log lay 12 steps in front of Dad's blind. When the gobbler reached the log, he suddenly squatted and disappeared again. Dad quickly raised his 3-inch Model 12 Winchester pump shotgun with a relieved, I've-got-you-now feeling.

You know how it is, don't you, when you are cradling nine pounds of 12 gauge dead weight and a gobbler decides to freeze behind a tree? After three minutes like that, the trembling began in Dad's arms.

He endured the pain for as long as possible, then lowered the gun as slowly as he could. He relaxed his arms for a full minute, then again lifted the heavy shotgun into shooting position.

After considering for two minutes every imaginable scenario that would explain the turkey's disappearance, Dad panned his gaze slowly to the left, then to the right, reassuring himself each time that there was *absolutely no possible way* the turkey could escape from either end of the log, without being fully visible.

Just as the agonizing situation was about to get the better of both his patience and his muscle endurance, Dad beheld a wattle-enshrouded head with a circumference as large as his shin suddenly pop like a submarine periscope up from behind the log.

Before Dad was able to slowly swing his shotgun that way, the massive longbeard began to casually amble away from the log, having somehow satisfied himself, while hidden behind it, that neither hen nor predator occupied the territory on the opposite side.

At first, Dad was unable to shoot, because he refused to take anything but a clear head or neck shot. The gobbler's head slinked down in front of him as he walked away, and he stopped occasionally to peck something on the ground, lowering the head even farther.

With a composure born of so many years in similar circumstances, Dad patiently waited for the proper moment to execute the shot. When the gobbler was 19 steps from the blind, he paused and instinctively raised his head to survey his surroundings. Dad's gun, which had been tracking the bird like guided-missile radar, fired immediately.

Dad was slightly disappointed when he picked the bird up. The gobbler had hypodermic-class spurs, but his beard was thin and he only weighed 16-½ pounds. He had seen that before, however. Some of the most dominant fighters prove to be grizzled old gobblers that are declining and losing bulk, but can still whip all the younger gobblers.

A deserving nominee for the Hall of Fame was that gobbler. He was nominated not only because it required almost an entire season for Dad to bag him, but also because possibly no other gobbler on the island ever compelled a hunter to endure mental agony and arm-cramps longer.

## Chapter 12

# GETTING SOME ZZZs

In my youth, the only people my age in the Delta who hunted turkeys were the sons of the original group of OK Hunting Club members. When I went away to college in the hills of east Mississippi, I met a small new group of contemporaries who were also interested in the sport.

In the sixties, there were only two or three areas in Mississippi where decent populations of wild turkeys were found. One of these areas was in southeast Mississippi around the town of Meridian, and that is where all of my new turkey-hunting acquaintances hailed from.

The first hill turkey hunter I met was Willie Clyde Green. His dad, Mr. Ed Green, was a friend of old Mr. M. L. Lynch, and had introduced Willie to turkey hunting at a tender age.

Mr. Green made turkey calls, too. He made a fine cedar slate-call and a variety of strikers, from long, hand-carved wooden ones to shorter wooden pegs glued into plastic-encased corn cobs.

I know some old-time turkey hunters who, even though they have dispatched dozens of turkeys, are still just as bloodthirsty as a 15-year-old. I know some who still have a hint of outlaw in them. They tote rifles, where legal, and won't hesitate to knock a gobbler off a limb with one at first light. They don't think twice about passing up jakes, even in years of low populations. They have no concept of preservation of the resource. Mr. Green, however, was a classic purist and conservationist of the wild turkey. When I first met him, in the late '60s, he had retired from hunting and hung his gun over the mantel for the last time, but thoughts of wild turkeys still filled his mind.

*The author and Willie Clyde Green with a "double" taken in 1976*

Willie Clyde told me once about the time that he and some local friends came into Mr. Green's neighborhood grocery during the spring turkey season, and jokingly remarked that they had jumped a hen off her nest and intentionally broken all her eggs. Mr. Green huffed, swelled up, and started turning beet red before Willie told him it was a joke.

It was in the spring of 1968 when Willie Clyde came to Ship Island for the first time to hunt turkeys. We both left school one Friday and made the 162-mile trip together over to Tunica. It was midseason. The weather had warmed and the mosquitoes were terrible.

Before leaving, I had briefed him about our bad mosquitoes and advised him to bring along some skeeter dope. I mentioned the mosquitoes again when we arrived in Tunica, and asked him if he had brought the stuff. He simply stated that he had, and I gave it no more thought.

We dropped Willie on the Roman Road the next morning, near its intersection with Tunica Cutoff Road. Backwater was in Earnheartsville Slough northeast of him, paralleling the ridge he was on, and we told him that we knew that some turkeys were roosted there.

Of course, it was still black dark when we arrived, and I couldn't see all of his gear when he climbed out of the back of the Bronco. He asked me to walk around to the front to help spray him in the lights of the vehicle.

My jaw fell when I saw what he had brought with him. There in his left hand was an old-timey pump sprayer. You know, one of those 24-inch-long contraptions that you used to see on the little table by the screen-porch door at your great aunt's house when you were a kid. It consisted of a screw-on can, on top of which was affixed a long cylinder containing a wooden-handled pump shaft.

Willie Clyde handed the device to me and requested that I fog down his hat, coat, and pants legs. Then he took a deep breath, held it, and squinted his eyes.

I began pumping, and soon the visibility was so low that the only way I could see the Bronco through all the haze was by its glaring headlights. I stopped when I thought I had vaporized him enough, but he held his coat up like a skirt and told me to keep spraying his shirt, front and back.

When he finally decided that the smog index 35 miles away in Memphis had been elevated sufficiently, Willie stepped off the road and melted into the dark Ship Island lushness.

I don't remember any of the details of my hunt that morning, but I'll never forget the tale that Willie Clyde narrated when we picked him up at noon, and this is it, just as he told it.

After the Bronco had slowly rolled off down the Roman Road, he penetrated the woods and stopped on the ridge west of Earnheartsville Slough. He waited for the black to start turning gray, and, when it did, he heard several gobblers crank up over the slough. He immediately moved to within 150 yards of the nearest gobblers, set up, and started to call.

Willie had one of the finest pieces of turkey hunting equipment I ever saw. His mother, a proficient seamstress, had made a hunting vest for him, completely customized to his specifications.

Willie Clyde, like a lot of hill turkey hunters, carried a fantastic number and variety of calls for that era: several different types of slates, with multiple strikers for each one; diaphragm mouth yelpers; and several types of wingbone and suction callers.

Willie's customized vest had a pocket sewn in it for every one of his calls, and each pocket was precisely the right depth and width for its individual call. Of course, the fabulous vest also had capacious side pockets for shells and lots of other items as well. None of the current, mass-produced hunting vests you see advertised in magazines could approach it for practicality.

While performing his calling routine early that morning, Willie used all of the multifarious calls in his vest, to no avail. The gobblers and their accompanying wenches all sailed down away from him to the east, to the ridge on the opposite side of the slough. His appetite had been whetted, however. He'd heard more gobbling than he had ever heard in one place at one time before.

Willie couldn't see any of the birds after they pitched down, but he sat and listened to the gobbling and associated hen talk across the water from him until it ceased an hour later. He waited, calling occasionally for an hour more. After concluding that the birds had drifted down the opposite ridge, he packed-up and decided to take action.

He struck the edge of the backwater after a hundred steps and since it didn't look deep to him, decided to cross to get on the same side with the immense flock of birds. He began to pick his way through the knee-deep slough, hoping that he wouldn't step into a cottonwood stump hole and draw the attention of the birds with his splashing.

He had maneuvered almost half way across the 80-yard-wide slough when his eyes detected faint movement on the opposite side. He instinctively froze and observed a hen grazing toward him almost imperceptibly along the water's edge.

Thinking that the whole flock might be following close behind her, he elected to sink down into a sitting position in the cold water next to a small hackberry tree.

Of course, from his new position the water was no longer knee deep, but was over waist deep, and when he looked down he saw that two thirds of the call pockets on his mama's vest were submerged in the swamp water.

In the month of April, Mississippi River backwater, much of it originating from northern snow-melt, has not had time to warm much above 50 degrees, and the initial shock of the water took his breath.

In spite of the discomfort he felt, Willie was soon delighted that he had sat down, for coasting along 15 steps behind the uninterested hen came a fanned-out longbeard. Willie speculated about the distance to the water's edge along which the turkeys were walking, and concluded that it was just beyond killing range. Willie knew he was in a tenuous situation, and he debated his options. He concluded that he had two. One was to grit his teeth, endure the cold, and keep alive his chances for a gobbler. He thought he would have an opportunity to move to the ridge when the turkeys finally ranged away from him out of view.

The second option was to wade to the ridge as fast as he could, sit down on the edge of the water, hope that they didn't spot him, and that they would continue to work their way to him.

Choosing the latter option would relieve the pain caused by the frigid water, but the water would probably slosh too loudly as he waded to the bank and run the birds off for good. Recklessly running turkeys away was anathema to him, so he chose to stay-put.

As is routinely the case in the sport of turkey hunting, Willie Clyde's wait was not brief. Any seasoned turkey hunter knows that wild turkeys do not hurry. They usually move about as fast as glaciers.

It took the strutting gobbler and the hen 35 minutes to peck and scratch along the water's edge to a point even with Willie. Even at that point, they were still out of range of his three-inch 12 gauge.

As he sat there motionless in the chilling water, Willie began to notice that the cardinal and wren tweets he had been hearing all morning were being masked by an intense zzzeeeing sound. He was even more aware of the multiple mini hypodermic-like pricks that he was beginning to sense on his face.

He also remembered wondering, while enroute earlier, why the rest of us, in addition to applying flying insect-killer spray to our clothing as he had done, had been applying repellent to every part of our anatomy where there was exposed flesh. Simply fogging his clothes with his sprayer had always been good enough in the hills.

Willie had enough presence of mind to realize that he shouldn't do any calling. He gave turkeys credit for more sense than that. No self-respecting gobbler would come to a call made by a hen standing in two-foot-deep water, 40-plus yards out from the bank of a slough. He knew the only thing he could do was to patiently stay focused on the turkeys at the water's edge.

Occasionally, Willie allowed his gaze to fall on the

swamp water he was sitting in. After looking down several times, he began to notice tiny squiggles on the water's surface. He watched more closely, trying to determine what the squiggling things were. Soon he began to observe that the squiggles were writhing larvae, which were turning into pupae before his eyes. Then he noticed that the pupae were transforming into adult mosquitoes, which fluttered from the water's surface to add reinforcements to the aerial assault on his tormented epidermis. It was quite a living laboratory, and Willie suddenly realized that he was witnessing the complete life cycle of the Mississippi River Delta mosquito.

Following along 40 yards behind the first gobbler and hen were the other members of the flock Willie had heard earlier on the roost. Sixteen other turkeys formed the group: four other long-bearded gobblers, two of which strutted almost continually, three jakes, and nine hens.

Over the two-hour period that Willie sat in the water, all of the turkeys milled up and down the bank of the slough from the point opposite him to no more than 40 yards up and down the bank in both directions.

Once during the turkey convention on the ridge, he saw a hen vanish from sight into what he surmised was a stumphole. She stayed down in the hole for an inordinately long time; so long that he wasn't even sure that she was in a stump hole. His deluded mind began to think that maybe she had entered the Twilight Zone, or a fourth dimension.

Willie Clyde never got a shot at a gobbler that morning, but blessedly, the entire flock eventually pecked and strutted off into the woods of Earnheartsville, perpendicular to the slough, and gave him some relief.

Willie was a hardened hunter, and he gamely sloshed over to the east side of the slough and set up on dry land after they had moved away. By then, however, the birds were irreversibly headed to parts unknown.

When we met Willie on the road at noon, his eyeballs were showing a lot of white, due to the excitement of hearing and seeing that many turkeys together. His breathing was shallow as he explained to us what had happened to him.

Willie came to Ship Island for two or three years before he killed his first turkey there, but after he learned his way around the terrain, he had regular success. He and I even doubled on longbeards in the same day a couple of times.

Willie hasn't been back to the island for many years now. When I last talked to him on the phone, he'd quit hunting, bought some pasture land, and become a weekend rancher.

Later, I thought of something I forgot to mention to him on the phone. I think I'll call him back sometime and discuss it with him. I want to tell him that if he ever has a yard sale, to go ahead and sell his old sprayer, but if he sells any old clothes, to advise me first. There's an old vest I want to buy from him.

## Chapter 13

# DRILLING FOR GOBBLERS

Another hillbilly friend from Meridian, Mississippi, Billy Brookshire, has hunted on Ship Island for many years. Billy is due much of the credit for this book coming into existence. When we were in college, I noticed one day that he was writing notes in a small journal, and I asked him about it.

He told me that the journal contained accounts of all of his turkey hunts. He said he was planning to write a book on turkey hunting someday, and the stories in the journal would serve as the basis for the book.

That struck me as a neat thing to do, and, from that day on, I started keeping my own journal. I figured that, even if I never got around to writing a book, at least the records would help me to even the odds a little bit with the wild turkey.

I kept a journal for 25 years before finally consolidating its entries into book form, but the details of the hunts described within it started making me a better turkey hunter only a few years after its inception. I discovered that details such as temperature range, dew amount, sky condition, moon phase, and other particulars about the weather are of great value to have for reference. With this type of information, a hunter can begin to discern patterns in gobbling amounts and other wild turkey behavior.

One of the most important details to record, especially for those of us who hunt in a floodplain, is river-gauge levels. That one item has probably had as much impact on my hunting success as anything else, including descriptions of how I worked turkeys and what types of calls I made to them. Notations about the amount of flooded and unflooded area at each gauge level can save a hunter a lot of time and effort, because he'll always know exactly where to go no matter what the gauge reading is.

I always write as much as I can about every hunt, and often I wind up with two or three pages of notations. It can be a chore after a hunt to stop and make a record of it, and sometimes I have to force myself to do it, but it has made my turkey hunting experiences more meaningful.

Like Willie Clyde Green, it took Billy Brookshire a couple of years before he figured out swamp turkeys, but he's had good luck ever since. He, like Willie, uses a wide assortment of wingbones and suction yelpers, slates, mouth calls, and friction calls, but he's the only turkey hunter I've ever known who confessed to lying down on his stomach to call turkeys.

When Billy first visited the island, in 1972, it was still legal in Mississippi to use a rifle, and he brought with him an expensive German-made drilling, with two 12-gauge barrels over a 7mm rifle barrel. He retired it to the cabinet later because it became too valuable to be used out in the woods.

Apparently, his drilling and his lying-down technique had served him well in the pine hills, but they caused him problems the first time he came to Ship Island.

I dropped him off at the intersection on Roman Road early in the morning of his first visit, and continued down into the north end of Big Bend to hunt.

At midmorning I heard a shot sequence from Billy's area that transmitted a message as clearly as Western Union: *Boooom......... Boooom.....................keouwwwwwww.* I wouldn't have known the details better if I had seen them on the 10 o'clock news.

I was waiting at the intersection when Billy came out of the woods at noon, shoulders slumped. I told him that I was pretty sure what had happened, but I wanted to hear it anyway. He described working a fine gobbler off the roost and having him hang up out of range with hens. He patiently continued to work on the bird, using every call in his coat, and finally enticed him into shotgun range, he thought.

Billy disdained using the 7mm, choosing the 12-gauge tubes instead. After the initial shot, the gobbler appeared to make his escape unhurt, and Billy emptied his second 12-gauge barrel. Still unscathed, the massive bird lifted off the ground and flew. Billy's third and last shot was simply a Hail Mary at 90 yards with the 7mm, as the gobbler was flapping through the forest canopy.

Afterwards, Billy stepped off 60 paces to where the gobbler had stood. When he finished describing the details to me, I naturally asked him why such an experienced turkey hunter would take such a distant shot. He explained that it was because he had been lying-down on his stomach, and the flat, unfamiliar terrain fooled him.

Brookshire missed another gobbler before he abandoned the habit of "bellying-up" to birds in the Delta, and he eventually became accustomed to the flat woods. He's killed several nice gobblers on the island since then.

Brookshire hunts more places than anybody I know. He hunts a couple of places in Georgia, at least four different places in Alabama, at Tunica, and around Meridian, Mississippi. As any traveling turkey hunter will tell you, it's real tough to consistently pattern and kill turkeys when you move from region to region like that. Brookshire, however, has had remarkable success doing it; that is, ever since he quit lying down and drilling for his gobblers.

## Chapter 14

# 1987—What A Year!

## The Kind Of Problem I'd Like to Have

In our region, the wild-turkey hatch typically occurs in late May or early June. A high river level at that time is usually devastating to the turkey population. The full effect of a late flood on the number of mature gobbling birds is not felt until a year or two later, but nonetheless is distressing to us serious hunters.

Abnormally high May and June river levels plagued us in both 1983 and 1984. Our hatches those springs were well below-normal, and hunter success, in terms of total numbers killed, plummeted in 1985 and 1986.

I've observed during years of low populations that it's generally easier then to call up old gobblers. I emphasize the use of the word "generally," because you can still occasionally run into calloused old gobblers with high I.Q.s.

Our population was at one of the lowest points ever during 1986, but that year I was able to call up a higher percentage of the old gobblers that I located. I'm sure it was due to less competition; after all, after a die-off, there are less hens in the woods, too. I've been through several up-and-down cycles, and the down years in the cycle are depressing every time they come around. It's always the same. You don't hear much. Seldom is there a gobble, and, if there is, it's way-off somewhere in the distance.

You don't even hear any hens or jakes chattering on the roost. You don't see sign—no feathers or droppings in the woods, no dusting places, no scratching, and none of the most significant sign, tracks on wet roads.

If there aren't any tracks, you can be fairly confident there aren't any turkeys. Maybe a turkey can slip unseen like a specter below the tops of the poke salad in the woods, and maybe, when you don't see scratching, the turkeys are feeding on buds and emerging foliage. But there just ain't no way a turkey can stop its toes from mashing down the mud when he crosses a wet road.

I've read statements by biologists that hatching success rises when turkey populations are lowest. The year 1985 was one of several that I personally observed that to be true.

It seems to be so that, concerning both man and wildlife, the Lord will provide. Just when you're about to give up hope, and you think the turkeys are history, you get surprised, and soon you're worrying about overpopulation and disease again.

We noticed a large number of jakes and yearling hens in the spring of 1986, but there was so little gobbling activity that we figured it would be a couple of years before we would enjoy quality hunting again. We theorized that in 1987 our turkey population would be comprised almost exclusively of two-year-old gobblers.

We also theorized that the twos would gobble well, unlike most years when they are stomped-on by a normal population level of old gobblers. But, boy, were we surprised, because 1987 was the best year in my memory for old gobblers on the island.

In my turkey-hunting journal I have a page or two after the last spring hunt that summarizes each season. The 1987 summary states: "Unbelievable how many more gobbling birds we had than last year, and most of the birds killed were three years old, indicating we had a much better hatch in 1984 than we'd originally thought. Only five jakes total were seen by all the hunters combined on the island in 1985. Last year's fantastic crop of jakes was practically invisible as two-year-olds this year (1987). Apparently, there were enough three-year-old gobblers (which hatched in 1984) to completely intimidate the large crop of two-year-olds and keep them quiet this year."

The experience of the spring of 1987 reinforces something that I've seen occur a couple of other times. When population levels are lower than normal, there's less gobbling by the surviving gobblers, and you can easily be tricked into thinking that the population level is lower than it actually is.

I certainly don't represent myself as a biologist, but I think this phenomenon results from a God-given protective mechanism in the wild turkey's nature. Apparently, when there is a decrease in population, the surviving turkeys sense it, and they gobble less, become more suspicious, and are more difficult to call successfully.

A couple of times in the spring of '87, I was forced to walk away from a gobbling bird only minutes after shooting another one. One such time was at the Red Line Road, on April 17. I was able to call in a 17-½-pound, three-year-old gobbler straight off the roost, and shoot him at 6:43, daylight saving time. After I picked the bird up, I decided to hang him up and pluck him on the spot before he got cold and his feathers took a set. Only a few minutes after my shot, while I was plucking the first bird, I began to hear gobbling only 150 steps north of me. I kept on plucking, but soon noticed the gobbles were getting closer.

I temporarily stopped my work, moved closer to the gobbler, and sat down. I halfheartedly began to work the bird, with no intention of shooting him. I was certain he'd soon hang up, and when he did, I planned to leave and resume my plucking job.

I could tell only a few minutes later that the gobbler wasn't halfhearted at all. Though he moved slowly, he steadily closed ground on me. I knew I wasn't going to shoot him, and I began to think about how I might unnecessarily educate him and make him harder to call up in the future.

By the time I'd decided to discontinue my efforts, the gobbler had approached so near to me that I was afraid he might spot me if I walked away. I was eventually forced to crawl on my stomach back to the thicker area where my half-naked bird was.

After I had fetched the dead bird, I could still hear the second one gobbling as I walked back to my vehicle.

I'll bet I've made 500 gobblers walk away and leave me in my turkey hunting career. It's an easy thing to do. But it's surprising how hard it is when the roles are reversed and you have to walk off and leave the gobbler instead. I've had very little experience with that sort of thing, but I'd like more chances to learn about it, because it's the kind of problem I'd like to have.

## UMBRELLA FEATHERS

I had another delightful hunt in 1987, on the morning of April 5. That day dawned clear and calm, with a low temperature of 35 degrees and light frost. We had a lot of guests hunting the prime spots in the main woods that day, and I planned to take the leftovers. I stood in the middle of Bailey's Big Field before light and listened for a gobble in any direction.

From the field, I would be able to hear turkeys in three different areas unoccupied by hunters: Paw Paw Ridge, The Airstrip Woods, and the Levee Board's wooded borrow pits, on which our hunting club controlled the hunting rights.

The borrow pits are areas along the base of the river levee where, many years ago, the levee builders "borrowed" the dirt used for constructing the levee. These pits were usually dug by dragline, and they generally vary from about six to twelve feet deep. Most have timber in them, but occasionally some were dug deeper and hold water for most of the year. During spring seasons when the river behaves, a few turkeys use these pit areas, and both they and hunters can move through the borrow pits just like the other woods on the river side of the levee.

After straining my ears for a few minutes, I finally heard one remote gobble to the east before fly-down time. I hustled that way, and discovered that the gobbler was roosted over the borrow pits just off the North Cottonwood Field, east of Frederick Bayou. I quickly set up down in the dry borrow pit, just off the east side of the field. There was just enough time left for me to make one yelp before the birds left the roost, and it roused a strong gobble.

Once the birds were down, I was able to discern two different gobblers. They both strode quickly up to within range of my blind, using an avenue of approach that was behind the only heavily-limbed, fallen tree top in my field of vision.

How uncanny it is that turkeys often seem to instinctively use available cover to conceal their movement. It's a great testimonial to their survival skills.

When a dominant gobbler makes his move toward a hen (or caller), he'll usually stop before reaching her, extend his head vertically to survey for her, and then often display. He usually won't come all the way to her at once, but will stop and allow the hen to make the final approach.

The gobbler, however, usually won't give her long to do this, and if she doesn't appear, will usually depart after only a few minutes of offering her the opportunity to join him. This behavior is probably due to a genetic trait that protects the species from predators.

Typically, once the gobbler has made his exodus, it's difficult for a hunter to turn him and call him back. It can be done, but these attempts fail more often than they succeed. The caller is probably better advised to move and get rounders on the bird, if the terrain allows it.

The above discussion of typical turkey behavior accurately describes what happened to me that morning. The two gobblers strutted a few minutes behind the thick treetop, during which time I witnessed two hens sail down from nearby trees to join them.

Soon afterwards, I glimpsed through the thick area a longbeard and a hen slowly promenading away through the relatively open borrow pits to the south. They faded from view, and I knew from the ever-more-distant gobbling of the male that they were leaving me.

I quickly exited the borrow pits, made a rounder to the south, re-entered the borrow pits, and set up again. I called for 90 minutes, to no avail.

It was Sunday, and I left the woods earlier than normal to go to church. Instead of returning to my vehicle along the shorter path north through the borrow pits, and risk spooking the birds, I retraced the steps I'd taken when I'd made rounders earlier.

I was walking slowly down a dirt road, and just before it entered the south end of the field where I'd set up at daylight, I stopped to survey the field. When I walk a road, I always attempt to walk on the shady side of it whenever possible, and the habit paid off for me that day.

As I stood in the shade of the road where it entered the southwest corner of the field, my eyes detected the slight movement of a black object 300 yards away, near the northeast corner. After studying it, I discerned a lone, ostrich-size gobbler slowly meandering and feeding there, oblivious to my presence. He was grazing north, getting steadily closer to the northeast corner of the small field. I stood there motionless until he entered the woods, at which point he descended out of view into a dry, narrow slough running east and west along the north side of the field.

As soon as the gobbler disappeared I sprinted the 300 yards to the northwest corner of the field, which was a hundred yards from where he had entered the deep slough. I gambled that the gobbler, instead of moving east into the borrow pit area, would migrate west along the bottom of the slough toward me.

Knowing that I might not have a long wait, I simply knelt in the shade beside a small tree on the bank of the slough.

I made one series of yelps with a mouth call, then three series of jake gobbles on my snuff-can caller. There was no answer. Only a couple of minutes after calling, I was focusing intently on the bottom of the slough when I heard a faint, strange sound to my left.

I slowly diverted my gaze left, and there, less than 20 yards away on the opposite bank of the slough, was the black gobbler, standing motionless, blown up like a frog's throat. I watched from the shadows as he folded up his feathers and popped back into a strut three different times.

The sound I'd heard was the sound of his feathers popping out as he went into his strut. It was quite an unusual sound, reminiscent of the sound an umbrella makes when it pops open.

I wasn't sure if I had ever heard that sound in the woods before. Maybe I'd heard it at a distance but didn't notice because it was so indistinct. I think I've heard it maybe once since then, but it's a sound that has to be made from nearby to be heard clearly.

When I heard the gobbler's strut sounds, I was reminded of the first time I heard drumming. In my youth, I listened to old hunters describe the sound of drumming for years before I could positively say I'd heard it myself.

The general consensus of the old-timers was that it sounded sort of like a truck stuck in a mudhole way off in the distance, briefly revving its engine as the tires spun.

After hearing that description, my mind would replay

the sound over and over while I sat in a blind. I would compare suspicious sounds I heard in the blind to the stuck-truck sound in my head, and hoped that some day I would be able to positively state that I had heard a gobbler drumming.

It was easy for me to recognize that sound after I had positively identified it the first time. In my opinion, it's still the most exciting sound you can hear in turkey hunting, even more exciting than a gobble. The reason I think so is because when you hear drumming, you know the gobbler is real close.

Drumming can only be heard about 70 or 80 yards away in our bottomland-hardwood tracts, and that's on a day when the wind is calm. I've noticed that I can only hear it about 30 to 40 yards away when the wind is blowing 15 m.p.h. or more. It can be heard a little farther away in upland pine/hardwood tracts.

Another reason drumming gets my attention is because, according to biologists, only mature gobblers make the sound, so you know a big boy is interested in you when you hear it.

Well, enough digression. Back to Umbrella Feathers. The big fellow hadn't noticed me as I knelt there in my shady spot. The trees surrounding him were just barely large enough to allow me to raise my shotgun when he passed behind them, without him spotting the motion.

He soon glided behind one of the small trees while fully fluffed out in a strut, and I was barely able to snap my gun into ready position before he broke the plane of the tree's opposite side.

I shot the three-year-old, 20-½-pound bird at 20 steps.

That hunt was one of my more bizarre ones, but old Umbrella Feathers was the fourth largest gobbler I've ever taken.

## THE SULTAN OF THE SLOUGH

The spring of 1987 was also the spring that I encountered what was to become a legendary member of what I call my All-Time-Hardest-To-Call Gobblers Society.

I didn't locate the gobbler until the season was almost over. The story began on the afternoon of April 19. I was moving along the east side of The Slough, a shallow depression that begins just north of our south line and extends south down on Seabrook land. I was essentially scouting for the next morning's hunt and didn't expect to hear any gobbling. Nevertheless, I was calling every 200 steps, and was surprised when I got a confident gobble from the west, across The Slough from me. I moved through the dry upper end of The Slough and set up on the other side. I flushed one of the gobbler's hens away as I went to him, but he continued to gobble.

As I moved to him, I didn't know that I was about to encounter one of the most guileful gobblers I have ever seen. I worked him that first afternoon from 1:40 to 7:18 p.m.

His gobbling was infrequent, only once or twice an hour, but he had the most thunderous and commanding gobble I've ever heard. His voice reminded me of my Army drill sergeant, whose bellowing voice would cause my head to snap back when the sound waves from his rebukes reached my ears.

A select-cut logging job in 1985 had littered the area with tree tops and that old bronze brute used them well to his advantage, exhibiting an uncanny knack of consistently selecting the appropriate top or thicket to conceal his approach. His ability to do this was so exceptional that it led me to conclude that it was not simply born of instinct, but rather raw, native intellect.

The gobbler's authoritative voice and wise nature lent an air of royalty to him. My imagination likened him to a sultan ensconced on his throne, surrounded by his subjects, and I christened him The Sultan of The Slough.

On one occasion that first afternoon, The Sultan stood within shotgun range for two hours behind two impenetrable tops in front of me, drumming incessantly but seldom gobbling.

He had reached his position behind the tops by taking a rounder on me. He had come from the south, circumnavigated me, and wound up at my right rear. I was able to discreetly shift around in his direction after he made his rounder.

I would have been able to shoot him if his subsequent approach had been in a straight line, because there was a clear path directly in front of me. But he instead quartered off to my flank, using the tops as interference.

My attempts to lure him while he stood behind the tops were fruitless. After two hours, his gobbles grew more infrequent and faint, and it became apparent that he was beginning to drift slowly away to the south line again. By then it was 6 p.m., daylight time, and I surmised that he was thinking roost.

The woods had thickened in the luxuriance of late spring, which facilitated my making a rounder on him as well. I made my circle, set up 10 yards north of the south line, facing south, and began to call with yelps and jake gobbles.

One of the yelps rekindled The Sultan's interest, and he began to gobble more than he had at any other time that afternoon. He moved to my right, then to my left, to the east edge of the water in The Slough. Then along the water he came north toward me. I thought I had picked a setup spot that afforded me adequate control of the water's edge, but, somehow, before I knew it, he wafted like an apparition past me to my left rear. Either he had shrewdly used what cover there was to veil himself as he passed by, or else he was invisible.

I knew it when he had passed, because he gobbled when he reached my left rear, as if to taunt me. I could hear him moving away farther north, so I shifted around my tree again to face him. Dusk was growing near, and I felt certain by then that he was headed to roost.

It was semidark when I departed at 7:18. Because I was so sure The Sultan had roosted north of me, I felt constrained to make a wide rounder to the west, via the South Line Road, to avoid spooking him.

Tranquil winds and glimmering skies greeted me the following morning. A spring heat wave was upon us. The high temperature reached 90 degrees later in the day.

The Sultan was the only gobbler I heard at dawn. I recognized his bellicose gobbles. He was roosted over the South Line Road where I had walked out the night before. How I had been able to depart at dusk without spooking him is one of those mysteries I can't explain. He obviously hadn't gone north to roost, as I had expected him to.

I was so intimidated by the mystique of the bird that I considered throwing in the towel, but I decided to accept the challenge, instead, and went after him with renewed vigor.

I set up northeast of The Sultan, only 30 steps from the two tops he had used to his advantage in round one of our battle the previous afternoon. Just before fly-down time, I was surprised to hear two more birds that he had permitted to reticently gobble near him. There'd been no trace of them the afternoon before.

My strategy was to call from 300 steps away, move up under cover of the early morning darkness to within 150 steps, set up, and remain silent. I hoped to intercept The Sultan when he made the hang-up that I anticipated.

After light, all three gobblers sailed down together, alighted 100 yards from me, and moved not a step closer. I refused to call for an extended period after setting up, thinking they would move within range before hanging up.

Wild-turkey gobblers almost never behave as we who study them think they logically should, and these three were no different. When it became apparent they were not going to move closer, I gave up and began calling. I yelped and jake gobbled only, with my homemade box call and my snuff can.

After my calls commenced, the birds began moving in an arc from left to right. After witnessing them move across in front of me for 30 minutes, I increased the frequency of my calling and they slowly began to drift toward me.

It was dejavu as The Sultan lead his minions past me. They were in range, but veered to my left behind a screen of huge tops, as before, instead of approaching through the open corridor in front of me.

Their gobbling quieted when they passed behind the tops. While they were hidden from me, I was able to shift to my left and position myself for a possible shot when they stepped out at the other end.

Somehow, The Sultan led his attendants past me again, out of view under the tips of the scattered weeds at the end of the top. I knew it had happened when I heard the triumphant booming gobble 30 yards behind me that could only belong to The Sultan.

I recognized by the succeeding gobbles that they were moving north away from me. After they drifted far enough for me to move, I shifted and attempted to call them back, but couldn't turn them.

I never did kill that regal gobbler. My hunting journal states, "The gobbler acts human."

My most prominent recollection of him was his assertive gobble. I've also never experienced turkey behavior like his, before or since then. I've never had another gobbler come within range of me as often, and stay within range for as long as that one did, without my eventually having a good shot at him. I not only failed to get a shot at The Sultan, but never even caught a glimpse of His Highness.

## FALL CAN BE FABULOUS

The fantastic hatch of 1986 was followed by another prodigious one in 1987, and, by the fall of 1987, wild turkeys were almost as common as squirrels on Ship Island. In addition to wonderful spring hunting, those two consecutive successful hatches laid the foundation for the finest fall hunting I've ever experienced.

John Eddleman and I went to Ship Island on the afternoon of November 12, primarily to scout for the next morning's hunt. As is typical in the fall, we covered two large areas that afternoon but found very little sign.

My experience with fall hunting is that it is a hit-or-miss thing in the extreme. Turkeys are traveling in large flocks in the fall, and if you're lucky enough to make contact, you're in for a good time, because there will usually be a lot of birds in the area. But, because they're bunched-up in the fall, there are a lot of blank areas in the woods, too, and you can walk a cramp in your legs attempting to find turkeys.

John and I went out again the next morning, and scouted through the woods continuously until noon, looking for turkeys. I covered three miles of territory in Big Bend and along the Slash, and my only contact was with one lonely yearling jake, which I called up to 10 steps and didn't shoot.

Still determined to find birds, I continued my search in Earnheartsville, and finally located a group there late in the afternoon. I got a response to my lost calling, and started working up a flock of unknown size.

I remembered that Willard McIlwain was bringing my son Bob and his son Lee to camp that night, so I quietly slipped away and saved the flock for the next day.

I brought Bob back the next morning, with the intention of breaking up the flock while they were still on the roost, and calling them back together on the ground. When we reached the roost area, our eyes began to discern silhouettes of turkeys in practically every tree, against the dawning glow of the eastern sky.

We methodically began to wind our way through the area, playing reveille with our guns, to rouse the sleepy birds and scatter them from the roost.

After fragmenting the main flock, we spent several more minutes scattering the splinter groups and stragglers that had flown only short distances from the epicenter of the confusion. The flock seemed to hold 25 to 35 birds, and I was encouraged about the prospects of Bob killing his first turkey.

We set up in a blind facing northwest, encircled by two camouflage nets. Because the flock appeared to be a family flock, I began calling with kee-kees and lost calls only a couple of minutes after we had finished the blind.

Despite our ardent dispersal efforts earlier, the birds reunited near the west high bank of Old River, 80 yards north of us, and began to slowly wander away.

The predominant goal of the day was for Bob to bag his first turkey. The tactics required to do so were unimportant, as long as they were ethical and legal. I saw an opportunity to slip unseen below the high bank, circle the birds, and drive them back over Bob, old-fashioned style. I told him to slowly trail the departing flock and watch for them to flush back over him from the north.

I was able to accomplish my move quickly without the flock spotting me. As I mounted the high bank north of the birds, I noticed turkeys lifting off the ground in waves between Bob and me and flying in my direction. Bob had somehow made contact with them before I had finished my maneuver.

Squadron after squadron of turkeys rose in front of me. Since there was not enough distance between us for them to attain full altitude, many of the birds flapped by only a few yards over my head.

Even though both hens and gobblers may be taken in

the fall under Mississippi game laws, I had not personally intended to shoot a bird in a family flock. I was so focused on Bob getting his first turkey, that I resisted the temptation to shoot one until I'd watched about a dozen part my hair like opening day doves. At last I succumbed, and shot one of the plump young birds.

I've had to duck to avoid being hit by falling doves and ducks, but that was the only time I've had to duck a falling turkey. It hit the ground five or six feet behind me as I dropped to my knees to avoid it.

Though disappointed that our initial plan had failed, I wasn't discouraged, because we had just accomplished another excellent bust on the flock and were given a second chance to call them back to us.

After Bob joined me, we blinded up again at the approximate site of the second bust. Soon we had the divided bevies coming again from the north and west, and we also began to hear a new flock approaching with interest from the south, behind us. In the new flock we began to hear a mature gobbler, gobbling strong and often.

As we sat there, we began to hear even more family-flock talk as well. Another large family flock had thrown in with the first flock, and that entire section of Earnheartsville became the site of a major conclave of Tunica County turkeys. It was pure auditory delight and, without question, the most turkey talk I've ever heard in one place.

We heard boss hens and yearling hens clucking, yelping, lost-calling, and kee-keeing. We heard yearling jakes kee-keeing, yelping, a few barely gobbling, and some attempting to gobble.

And we also heard older gobblers yelping, clucking,

and gobbling.

According to biologists, old gobblers never associate with family flocks during the winter. I've personally seen long-bearded gobblers with family flocks, but they may have been year-and-a-half-old gobblers, last spring's jakes, which were still associating with siblings.

The gobbling we heard that morning was made either by these semi-mature gobblers, or by older gobblers in a separate flock proximate to the family flocks.

As the sun rose and the temperature warmed, the gobbling seemed to intensify. We heard 75 to 100 gobbles over the course of the hunt.

Several of the birds, including two of the older gobblers, had worked up almost to within shotgun range of us when a hen stepped from behind a top and offered us a shot at 15 yards.

Ordinarily I would have waited for one of the older gobblers, but I remembered the prime directive of the day, my son getting his first turkey. Any experienced turkey hunter will attest that a bird-in-range is worth far more than two behind the thicket, so I told Bob to take her. He emptied his gun, cut not a feather, and watched as the diminutive hen flew off.

I had no idea how many turkeys were in the area until after he'd shot. The subsequent activity reminded me of one of Alfred Hitchcock's sea gull attacks. Wing flapping and raucous putting ensued for almost 60 seconds before the woods again quieted.

My neck was bowed. I was bound and determined to get Bob a turkey. I was not sure how many times we could break up those same flocks, but I decided to move north 100 yards to the high bank of Old River, where the main concentration of birds had been, and set up again.

By the time we had completed our move, we were already hearing calls, and part of the flock had already reassembled in the woods north of us.

Not long after I began calling again, a satellite unit of the mother flock had moved to within shotgun range of us. Their approach, however, was just below the crest of the high bank, and we were unable to see them.

I continued to call, mimicking them, and three yearling jakes eventually ascended the bank. Bob shot one at 21 steps, and I breathed a sigh of relief. The pressure was off.

Just as my dad had done after my first kill, I carved a "B" on a box elder tree near the spot where the bird fell.

After reflecting on it, I concluded that what Bob and I encountered that day were at least two enormous flocks that were fairly proximate to each other. By chance, we had apparently been able to set up between the flocks and work all of them toward us.

We had assembled around us that morning the largest congregation of turkeys that I've ever been near, and the amount of gobbling was definitely the most I've ever heard on a fall or winter hunt.

John Eddleman, who was hunting on the ridge across Old River Lake from us that morning, said he could hear the gobbling clearly, and each time we scattered a flock, several birds flew across to his side. Once, one of the hens even alighted in a tree over his head and afforded him an easy shot.

Willard and Lee hadn't found any birds that morning, so when Bob and I met them for lunch, we gladly relinquished our Earnheartsville claim to them.

Immediately after entering the woods there, they made contact with some of the same birds and scattered them again. They were able to call up and rescatter the flocks several times over the course of the afternoon, missing two and killing two in the process.

When the day ended, the five of us had taken a total of five birds, the only time I remember a group that large batting a thousand on the island. The Earnheartsville flocks we pursued that day probably became the most-harassed flocks of turkeys to ever walk across Ship Island, but they sure provided us with an uproarious conclusion to 1987.

## Chapter 15

# Turkey Hunters 'Tween Twelve and Twenty

One of my first turkey hunting buddies was Kirk Biddle, a high-school classmate who took up turkey hunting with me in the days before it was popular with most of our peers.

Kirk and I had to rough it the first time we went to Tunica together, and were it not for the fact that Biddle was such a good sport, his turkey hunting career might have ended right there.

The motel was swamped with adult hunters on the night we arrived, and Kirk and I had to bivouac in the cramped back end of Dad's Jeep. The warmer-than-usual spring night necessitated our keeping the windows on the Jeep down, to the delight of the omnipresent mosquitos.

When the men woke us the next morning, we leapt with relief from our rudimentary vehicular beds, anxious to abandon them for the relative comforts of a turkey blind.

The first day that Kirk hunted at Tunica, I was his designated caller, a situation almost like the proverbial blind-leading-the-blind. A complete novice, Biddle had come to camp without necessities like calls and mosquito repellent (which we used to call mosquito dope, without embarrassment, until marijuana became common later).

I knew beforehand that he didn't have a turkey call and that I would have to do all the calling. What I didn't know, however, was that he didn't have any repellent, a particularly grave omission in Tunica County.

It's impossible to exaggerate how horrible mosquitos are on Ship Island when the river level is elevated in the spring. They rise in viscous clouds from wet areas as you pass through them, and I've sucked in the droning pests many times while breathing with my mouth open.

Repellent is as mandatory as a Mojave water-canteen, and a can of flying-insect-killer spray is desirable, to drive the infernal things from around your blind and stop the zzzz-ing so you can hear other sounds in the woods.

On Kirk's first morning, we located a gobbling turkey on Outhouse Ridge and set up to call to him. I positioned Kirk 15 yards in front of me and commenced calling to the bird on the roost.

In a nutshell, what happened was that I overcalled the gobbler. I know this now. He gobbled his throat sore, and, in my youthful exuberance, I responded to every gobble with another series of yelps. He finally decided to forsake what he thought was a too-bodacious hen.

Two other aspects of that hunt stand out in my mind. One is that it was the only time I remember having a bobcat come to my calling. I never actually saw the cat, but I know he was there. While I was working the gobbler I heard him scream five steps behind me.

I was alarmed enough to slowly unsnap my knife and pull it from its sheath, preparing for the possibility of the feline pouncing on me. Biddle was in front of me and farther away from the cat, but, as I remember it, he heard it scream, too.

The other prominent thing about the hunt was the torment I remember Kirk suffering from the mosquitos' unrelenting feeding frenzy on his face. He had been carefully warned about the keen eyesight of the wild turkey, so he valiantly struggled to be motionless, until he was compelled finally to rake the pests off his cheeks. That night he had the worst case of mosquito welts on his face I've ever seen. Some were the size of dimes.

Biddle eventually caught on to the sport of turkey hunting, and in 1981 killed one of the largest gobblers ever taken on the island. He killed it on an afternoon hunt, too, calling the 20-½ pound bird up at 5:55 p.m., standard time, only minutes after sitting down to call.

## Chapter 16

# TURKEYS ON THE TIP

John Eddleman started hunting on Ship Island a little over a dozen years ago. Eddleman is a man of many talents, a former Eagle Scout who can do everything from tying a bow line hitch to sculpting a fine box call from a piece of walnut.

In addition, he's a true sportsman and crafty woodsman, perfectly capable of navigating through strange woods in any type of terrain you set him in.

Though Eddleman started turkey hunting a little late in life, he rapidly improved to a point far beyond some who've hunted twice as long, and now he's quite accomplished at it. Once he was exposed to the sport, he became fascinated with it and even began making a lot of his own equipment. He's made several types of box calls, leather box-call holsters, chalk holders, shotgun-shell holders, and other gear.

John and I both like mouth calls and use them, but we've always been partial to box calls. At one point several years ago, we could not find a commercial box call that sounded loud enough and raspy enough to suit us, so we decided that we'd make our own prototypes. I pulled out some old blocks of walnut that I had, and we went to work. I made only a couple, but the new hobby captured Eddleman's interest, and he studied it and experimented until he learned how to make a perfect box call.

*John Eddleman and son, Kirk*

Since his first days on the island, when he was unfamiliar with the terrain and the peculiarities of Ship Island turkeys, he's had some of the most stimulating hunts a turkey hunter can have.

One of these adventures occurred in the spring of 1991, along the main road entering the island. While entering the island at mid-afternoon, we came around a sweeping curve in the Bronco and saw several dark objects in the middle of the road 400 yards west of us.

I slammed on the brakes, and we sat in the Bronco for 60 seconds, squinting into the sun and straining our eyes to make positive identification of the objects and to size up the situation.

Two of the objects were much larger and darker than the others, and we concluded that the group consisted of two old gobblers and four hens.

The birds were standing on the main road where it runs through a low area. The road there is a "fill-road," built up with fill dirt as much as 13 feet above natural ground elevation in places. The river was high, and the road was only a foot-and-a-half above the backwater which was lapping against its shoulders.

I knew the birds would not fly east to go to bed because there was not enough heavy tree cover in that direction to offer them secure roosts. To the east lay only a thinly forested borrow-pit area, the levee itself, and the cultivated cropland beyond the levee.

The wooded area from a point 300 yards west of the birds back to the levee a half-mile away was all under water. The road was high and dry except for a 30-foot-long low spot just east of the birds that was a foot under water.

In the opposite direction, the road extended westerly from the birds' location to where it joined the dry main ridge.

In effect, the birds were standing on the tip of a long, narrow peninsula of land, the road being the peninsula, extending from where it connected to the mainland of the ridge to the west, to the point where it was covered with water.

Within 3-½ hours it would be roost time, and it was obvious to us that the birds would move west along the road/peninsula to the main ridge when they decided to roost.

Stimulating thoughts flashed through my mind as we sat there for those 60 seconds. It was possibly the most perfect "hemmed-up" situation I've ever seen for turkeys, because we could predict their movement with relative certainty.

The situation afforded a man the opportunity to simply walk down the main ridge from the north, to a point just north of where the base of the road/peninsula joined the mainland of the ridge, and set up a blind. He could expect that within the three hours before roost time, the birds would almost certainly pass right by his blind beside the road. If a man cared nothing about the sport of it, the situation even offered a perfect opportunity to simply sit without calling and ambush the unsuspecting birds as they walked past.

The only thing that could possibly go wrong would be if the birds chose to fly directly off the tip of the peninsula and sail up to roost somewhere out over the backwater rather than to walk back to the ridge to fly up. We judged that to be unlikely, however, because the denser woods to the west offered far superior roosting.

After mulling these thoughts while observing the birds, we slowly retreated around the curve in the road. After we had disappeared from the birds' line of vision, we raced as fast as we could in reverse back to the entrance gate, then flew north along the gravel levee-top to Bailey's Woods. From there, we would approach the peninsula on the woods road along the east side of Old River.

The road through Bailey's was so torn up that it looked like a chocolate milkshake, and I chose not to put the Bronco through the torture of traversing it. I had already limited out, so I suggested to John that he hunt the six birds alone, then wished him luck as he started the trek through the mile-and-a-quarter of slop to the birds' peninsula.

I mentioned earlier that John is a sportsman, and, true to form, he chose the most ethical method of hunting the vulnerable birds. When he was 100 steps north of the main road, he stopped and blinded up along the edge of the backwater there, rather than assuming an ambush position alongside the road.

He built a thick blind from leafy box elder and hackberry limbs, sat down, and started calling on his homemade box call.

Eddleman sat there motionless for two long hours without hearing or seeing anything. He called infrequently, using only yelps and clucks.

He had set up initially at four o'clock, and the ever-diminishing angle of the sun over the two hours was beginning to concern him. Roost time was fast approaching. He kept worrying also about whether the birds would choose to fly up to roost farther east down the road, or, as he hoped, walk in his direction. He hadn't seen the birds, and he didn't know whether they were moving his way or not. If they were, the fact that they had not responded to his calling bothered him a little, but he shored up his confidence by reminding himself that in the afternoon turkeys often move to a caller silently.

John was finally able to raise a gobble from one of the gobblers with one of his raspy yelps, and it confirmed that they were indeed headed toward him. Soon, he was able to see their dim outline as they walked slowly west up the road. He saw only the two gobblers. Apparently the four hens had left the gobblers earlier and somehow passed by unseen.

When the gobblers reached the peninsula's base at the edge of the backwater, they turned north and took a few steps off the road toward John. His pulse quickened, but his excitement gave way to disappointment a couple of minutes later when the two longbeards turned and walked south, away from him.

Dusk was imminent and Eddleman, suspecting that the birds were headed to roost, knew his chances then were slim.

Nonetheless, he picked up a second box call, one he had hand-made using a Turpin box as a pattern, and, in desperation, made two loud series of lost calls.

One of the birds gobbled back in response that time, and they both wheeled and headed back to him. The silent bird was in the lead, and he marched straight to the decoy John had set in front of his blind.

Just as the lead gobbler approached within range, a

large whitetail deer grazed over between him and John. Eddleman had a marginally clear shot at the longbeard between the deer's legs, but he decided to risk waiting for a better shot in spite of his concern that the deer might spook the birds. The deer did wind him a few seconds later, but, luckily, it grazed away without snorting and exposed the first gobbler for an open shot.

My watch showed 6:46 when I heard the distant reverberation of John's three-inch 870. When I met him later, he was still hyperventilating over the experience. When he'd finished relating the story to me, we hurriedly cleaned the four-year-old bird before darkness descended.

The gobbler's crop was packed tight with yellow-top blossoms. Yellow-top is the local name for the groundsel plant, which grows in great profusion in areas exposed to plenty of sunlight.

We had noticed a patch of yellow-tops along the main road when we spied the birds earlier. We assumed that the birds were attracted to the tip of the narrow peninsula to feed on them. I don't understand, however, why they chose to feed on yellow-tops in such a vulnerable spot, when the plants grew prolifically all over the entire island. It's another of those little mysteries about wild turkeys. Sometimes they're unbelievably dumb-acting, and sometimes they astound us with their shrewdness. My experience has been that the latter is far more common.

## Chapter 17

# BULLY OF THE WOODS

Television is such a dominating influence now that most people can't imagine life without it. During the first eight years of my life, I can remember evenings spent with my family around the radio listening to programs like "The Shadow" and "Gangbusters."

During the daytime, I was forced to listen to my friends discussing what happened to Howdy Doody and Superman on television, because mine was the last house on the block to get one.

When one year I finally asked Santa for a T.V. and threatened to stop believing in him if it wasn't delivered, I became a member of the peanut gallery on Christmas morning.

One of the earliest shows I remember my parents watching on the tube was "The Naked City," a detective series set in New York City. The closing line for the show always went something like this: "There are eight million stories in this city, and you have just seen one of them." I've always remembered that great closing line, because it has been so applicable to most of my turkey hunts.

Often, after stumbling out of the woods at dark to meet a hunting buddy, having been thoroughly dispirited and humiliated by a bird with a brain weighing less than half an ounce, I've found myself saying to my companion, "There are eight million ways to *not* get a turkey, and I've just found another one."

Possibly the most frustrating of the eight million episodes are the ones where I've had the misfortune of meeting up with a bully gobbler.

Bully gobblers are tyrannical ruffians of the woods who have whipped all the other gobblers in the county so bad that they all quake with fear simply upon his appearance. It makes for an interesting scene when you run into one of these birds. You always go home entertained, but meatless. Allow me to give some examples.

One of the most enjoyable days I ever had also happened to be one of those days when I unknowingly encroached into the territory of a bully gobbler—May 3, 1980. The Mississippi Game and Fish Department had extended the spring season a few days past normal closing because of frequent inclement weather and a high river level during the season.

I went to Ship Island alone to hunt a final day. I walked to the Red Line Road and heard six different gobblers gobbling over the backwater east of me, and two more across Old River in Earnheartsville.

The woods were noisy. The river had fallen from its crest, and the leaves underfoot were dry and encrusted with silt from the muddy waters of the Mississippi. The predominance of sycamore trees in the area exacerbated the problem, because sycamore leaves are the largest, noisiest leaves in river-swamp woods.

I elected to approach the two nearest gobblers. To conceal the sound of my steps in the crackly leaves, I moved only when the birds gobbled, which, fortunately, was often. I tiptoed to within 125 steps, and put myself in the middle of a tangle of vines and lush, bushy growth next to a box elder tree.

I tree-clucked and yelped to the birds, and got good responses from both. After the gobblers sailed down from their roosts, they marched directly toward me, but hung up at the customary 60 steps.

As I studied the two birds, I began to hear two other gobblers steadily closing ground from the north. Before any of the four birds had time to work into shotgun range, a gobbler as tall as an emu materialized with four hens, 60 steps behind the original two birds.

I noticed the two hung-up birds suddenly come to attention and extend their necks to full length when the bully gobbler and his harem appeared. I could almost see their facial expressions turn to horror.

The two started running away from the bully, on a course that would bring them within 10 steps of me. I raised my gun, but the two birds were moving so rapidly that I was unable to get a shot off in time.

Of course, the movement of my gun alerted the emu-gobbler and his hens, and they putted a few times and melted back into the foliage behind them.

Despite the apparent glut of gobblers in the area, I moved a half-mile south to allow peace and harmony to return there before returning for what I hoped would be another round of adventure. I puttered around for an hour or so, then returned to the enchanted area and set up only 200 steps northeast of where my original blind had been.

My new blind was positioned where I'd heard the second pair of gobblers earlier, the ones that had been closing ground so rapidly toward me when the bully entered the scene.

Since I planned to stay there for the rest of the day, if necessary, I was much more thorough in constructing a blind than I had been earlier. The new blind required 25 minutes to build and was as thick as a Pterodactyl nest when it was finished.

After only four series of yelps, I heard a strong gobble response a hundred steps east of my blind. I stopped calling for a while, and the gobbler started drifting gradually to me, gobbling sporadically along the way.

He moved to within 55 steps, and was still closing on me from the east, but I was unable to see him because of the late-spring lushness. Suddenly a huge gobbler appeared south of me, trailed by four hens.

The swelled-up potentate stalked briskly toward the thick area where I'd last heard the poor gobbler that was slowly coming to my call. It was obvious that the stalker was the same pugnacious bully gobbler that had spoiled my earlier effort.

The first gobbler was of course never heard from again, and after he was evicted, the attacking gobbler and his hens again departed the scene as rapidly as they had earlier.

I sat there as the woods became silent again and reflected on the day's events. I was frustrated, but, at the same time, appreciated the privilege I'd had of witnessing secrets of the natural world that few folks are blessed to see.

I sat there in the blind calling for two hours more. To add insult to injury, when I finally decided to throw in the towel, and I leaned forward in my blind to pick up my equipment, a longbeard standing only 20 yards behind me spotted my movement, putted, and flew off.

Another prominent memory of a bully gobbler occurred on a late April day in 1983. An elevated river level had concentrated all the birds primarily on the ridge east of the Slash. Hal Winn and I boated to the Roman Road and heard at least 10 gobblers each, though some were distant.

He went to a hot gobbler that was roosted over the Slash, and I went farther southeast down the Roman Road. His bird didn't come off the roost until 9:30 a.m. and pitched west away from him to Outhouse Ridge, evidence that the birds had seen a lot of pressure on the narrow, confined ridges, because Hal is one of the most accomplished turkey callers I know.

I heard a good bird gobbling over the backwater, and went to him. I continued to walk the road to the point where it hit the water, then followed a contour line along the water's edge to a point between the bases of two narrow, 300-yard-long peninsulas of land extending from the main ridge like teeth on a comb.

The peninsulas were actually narrow hogback finger ridges extending off the main ridge we were on. The rising river had backed water onto the sides of the main ridge, and the two little hogbacks extended out into the water. Only 80 feet of backwater separated them.

I set up between the bases of the two peninsulas, 40

yards from the edge of the water, and began calling. I heard several birds sail down onto the peninsula to my left. They stayed in one spot for an extended period, presumably feeding and mating, and showed little interest in my calling.

I have seen birds do that before, when they cycle out of the mating urge late in the season and become more interested in loafing and feeding than in procreation. Another possible cause of this behavior is cumulative, season-long hunting pressure, and turkeys seem particularly sensitive to hunting pressure in high water situations. I've even seen them cease gobbling completely and sometimes remain on the roost all day when the pressure on river-confined ridges is too great.

For whatever reason, the turkeys moved glacially slow on the peninsula. It took them four hours to drift to me. Once during that time they hop-scotched the 80-foot distance from one peninsula to the other, and continued slowly approaching the mainland.

When they got into view, I saw a longbeard and two accompanying hens. As they were nearing the junction of the peninsula and the ridge, I spotted a second group of birds approaching on the main ridge farther south: four longbeards, two hens, and a jake.

As the three came off the peninsula, the group of seven joined them, and, at that point, they were all almost in shotgun range. I was planning my shot when Murphy's Law was actuated. I suddenly noticed every turkey neck in the entire gathering simultaneously extend in unison.

If you've ever observed a large group of turkeys together, you've seen that, typically, there will only be two or three on guard at any one time, with their necks extended, looking out for danger. If they all extend, you know something has gone wrong, because it's not natural for them to do this. Usually, they've spotted a hunter or a predator. But, in the case of the 10, they had spotted a bully gobbler.

Immediately after the members of the flock extended their necks, they began scurrying around in a completely disorganized manner.

I slowly shifted my gaze both left and right, and saw the source of their agitation. An enraged, fanned out dictator was tromping from my right rear directly toward them, as fast as his distended feathers would allow. He charged straight into the pack as they were attempting to escape. There was a brief thump and a smattering of vocal chatter, then the 10 were gone. They scattered over practically 360 degrees of the compass. It was one of the best bust-ups of a flock I ever saw, one a fall hunter would envy.

The bully departed the scene as promptly as he'd entered, presumably to return to a harem of coy hens skulking behind him. Out of a sense of duty, I aired a few plaintive gobbles, in the faint hope that I could reverse the course of the old bronze man, but with his mission accomplished, the brute ignored me and disappeared. The woods around me, which had been so alive with turkeys only seconds before, became lonely and mute again.

I've seen a lot of turkey fights and I don't ever recall one being advantageous to me. Some of these battles have been waged nearly within range of my shotgun. It seems to be characteristic of a turkey skirmish that all the participants and observers turn tail and evacuate the area when the melee is over, unconscious of everything else around them.

Before I knew better, I longed for chances to witness turkey battles, in the mistaken belief that it would make easy targets of the presumably preoccupied combatants and bystanders. I erroneously imagined it would be easy either to creep in on the birds while the fight was under way, or to call up departing birds after the battle was over.

After witnessing my first few turkey fights, I changed my mind about all this. Now I abhor fights. I hold my breath every time I work a gobbler, and hope he doesn't get drawn into one.

The only occasion when I got lucky in a situation where a bully gobbler intimidated another gobbler was in the spring of 1988, on a hunt in the Big Bend area of Ship Island. Failing to hear any roost gobbling, I set up to wait on a gobbler in a known strutting area.

Unbeknownst to either of us, John Webb and I had set up blinds within hearing range of each other. Two jakes came by me almost as soon as I had finished building my blind, and 25 minutes later I heard a gobble out in front of me, 200 yards to the south.

I cackled back to the distant gobbler, and he cut my call. After we volleyed back and forth a few times, I decided to stop calling. The bird closed rapidly, and when he was 45 steps from me he suddenly assumed the characteristic high-necked look of a startled turkey. He briefly came to attention, then fled by on my right, just out of range.

I strained to watch him as he ran to my right rear, and attempted to soothe him by clucking to him. He did stop running but continued to walk away until he was out of sight.

After waiting for two minutes, I yelped, and a gobble

from immediately behind me nearly blew my face mask off. I was lying on my back with my head propped against a large sycamore tree. Using the wide tree to advantage, I was able to carefully roll over behind it, without the bird on the other side spotting my movement. After I'd made my adjustment, I peeped cautiously through a dense tangle of vines growing along the sycamore's side.

The burly gobbler was only 15 steps away, slowly approaching me, in a full strut. I was able to lift my gun slowly and extend the muzzle of it through the vines without him seeing me. I shot him as he strutted, and when I did, two other black gobblers that had been silent winged away from behind him.

I shot the gobbler at a range of only 12 steps, and that was the only time I remember shooting a turkey's beak off. He was one of my all-time largest gobblers, a four-year-old weighing 20-½ pounds. He also toted an above-average-length beard for our woods, 10-½ inches.

When John Webb and I discovered back at camp that our hunting zones had overlapped, he related to me what he had seen.

He was building his blind when he heard the initial gobble. He looked up from his work and saw three longbeards trotting through the woods toward the gobbling bird. Only a few minutes later, he heard my shot.

We surmised that the following scenario had taken place: The gobble he heard was from the gobbler I had initially heard and called toward me. One of the three running birds he saw was a dominant gobbler, determined to banish the gobbling intruder. When the first gobbler spotted the three approaching longbeards, he spooked and left the area completely.

After the first gobbler departed, the bully gobbler evidently decided to commandeer the hen (me) for himself. He left his two comrades and approached my tree from the back side. The three gobblers had obviously circled me and approached out of my vision, but were spotted by the first gobbler.

I've had numerous other hunts ruined by turkeys fighting each other. Although it's an interesting phenomenon, sometimes I wish that it didn't come so naturally to them.

On the other hand, their fighting nature can actually be of more benefit than detriment, if we shrewdly use it to our advantage. The best way to do that is to pull out our favorite gobbling devices and challenge them to come fight us before they fight each other.

## Chapter 18

# TEMPERAMENTAL TORRENTS

Our favorite hunting ground, Ship Island in Tunica County, is a Mississippi River, bottomland hardwood tract located between the mainline protection levee and the river itself. Levees have been vital to man's existence in the flat Delta floodplain since the arrival of the pioneering settlers in the early 1800s.

The first levees were rudimentary ones, pushed up by individual plantation owners with slave labor and mule slips. The remains of some of the old slave levees can still be seen in a few places along the river.

No significant, organized levee work was accomplished until 1858, when the first levee district was formed. The levee district that includes Tunica County did not have a finished levee line along its river frontage until 1886.

Much of the land along the river front was cleared and

farmed before the interior lands because elevations near the river were generally higher. In pioneer days, flood water would inundate practically the entire Delta region, but after the levee districts were formed, the river was constricted in a narrow band with levees on each side. Levees contained the floods, but made the area between the levees more flood prone, despite generally higher elevations, than it had been in the pre-levee era.

Because of increased flood risk, hunters of lands "behind the levee" annually begin a flood watch in about late January each year, prior to the spring turkey season. Spring river crest levels may vary as much as 25 or 30 feet from one year to the next.

Most hunting clubs are unaffected when the river is at the lower end of that range, but at the higher end, some are forced to call off the spring turkey season altogether.

In the flat Delta region, a one-foot rise covers a surprisingly large number of acres, but if the river crests at an average or slightly above-average level, hunters can still have a decent spring turkey season. In fact, moderate flood levels can concentrate turkeys and add to the excitement of the spring season.

The concentrating effect of the river sometimes makes for wild and crazy hunts. A ridge where a hunter would normally hear four or five different gobblers on a decent morning might host 12 or 15 gobbling birds under flood conditions.

Hunting in such conditions sounds like it's a slam-dunk situation, but The Creator gave the wild turkey certain traits that compensate for its increased vulnerability in flood times.

It seems that the more concentrated wild turkeys are, the more vigilant and suspicious they are. When the size of their home territory is reduced, wild turkeys become more sensitive to the presence of man and the pressure he applies, not only by hunting activity but also by simply walking in the woods.

The first couple of days of hunting on constricted ridges are usually exciting, and hunter success is decent. After then, however, the success ratio usually declines noticeably, and by the end of the season, most adult gobblers will not respond at all.

Some of the best turkey hunters in our region have hunted with me at Ship Island during the latter stages of a flood, and they've consistently been skunked.

While kills may decrease over the course of a flood, the excitement level of hunts usually remains high until very late in the season. You're more likely to see turkeys during high water because they are hemmed up. And until pressure becomes too great, turkeys often continue to gobble well, and the gobbling is more concentrated. Gobbling is the most appealing aspect of turkey hunting to me, anyway. I've often told people that when I'm in the woods, I'm gobble hunting more than I'm turkey hunting.

Several floods have been devastating to spring turkey hunting and turkey populations on the island. The 1973 flood stands paramount; it was a flood of such magnitude and duration that we were unable to hunt on the island a single day during the entire six-week spring season.

One day that spring, Dad and I were motoring slowly in a boat on a flooded road on the island, just observing the effect the flood was having. We didn't have guns, of course, but we did have our box calls along with us.

We cut the motor in a couple of places, grabbed our calls, and simply scratched out a few yelps. Each time, we were greeted with anxious gobbling from several gobblers that were roosted on limbs somewhere out over the all-encompassing flood waters.

Because of the duration of the flood that year, those gobblers were prevented from leaving the roost for a period of a couple of months. Even though they must have known that there was no way they could mate hens (I've never read about gobblers treading hens on a limb), they were still apparently subject to procreative urges, and they gobbled readily at the suggestion of mating.

Severe floods, like the 1973 flood, apparently don't harm wild turkeys like they do other forms of wildlife. Turkeys can simply nip newly-emerging buds in the trees, and get along just fine until the waters recede. I've even seen turkeys choose to feed on buds rather than other soft mast available at ground level in unflooded conditions. I killed a big gobbler once that had a crop stuffed full exclusively with cottonwood buds.

The 1975 flood washed us out until the last weekend of the season. The flood waters covered our highest ridge and remained elevated through the time the trees leafed out. I saw one of the most unusual sights of my life on the island that spring.

The high-water mark on the trees from that flood was more clearly delineated than any I've ever seen. The line on the trees was about 30 inches above the tops of our highest ridges. Above the line, the foliage had grown to the verdant lushness normal for late spring, while below the line lay a bare, open moonscape covered with inch-thick, gray-black silt.

A man standing on a ridge with his head above the high-water line could see perhaps 30 or 40 yards through the dense foliage. If he knelt down, however, he could see for a breathtaking distance through stark, winterlike woods. The contrast was astonishing.

The '75 flood created the most unique environment for turkey hunting I've ever faced. When I traveled in the woods, I was unable to see turkeys very far away because of the junglelike lushness at eye level.

On the other hand, turkeys could easily see my legs moving at their eye level below the high-water line, and they would spook when I was still a great distance from them.

When I would sit down to call, I could see a long way through the woods also, but my green blinds stood out like beacons in the barren emptiness below the line.

We've had several other significant spring floods. The 1979 spring flood caused us to miss practically an entire turkey season. The 1983 and 1984 floods were rare back-to-back major-flood years, and our turkey population fell to the lowest level of my lifetime because of the poor hatches in their aftermaths.

No question, floods are unsettling to us turkey hunters. We need to have more foresight when they occur, however, because flooding does have a couple of benefits. One is that flooding during spring serves to check overpopulation and disease, a constant threat in prime river habitat.

A second benefit is that old gobblers seem to respond to calling more positively in the first spring following a severe flood. Never was this fact more evident to me than in the spring of 1974, the first spring following the quintessential flood of 1973. Occasionally, after nesting begins in a typical spring, it becomes easier to work some of the old gobblers that were formerly blanketed with hens. Late in a typical spring, those gobblers would be even easier to call up if it were not for yearling hens, most of which don't nest, but rather stay with the gobblers for the entire season.

In most years of severe flooding, hatching success is minimized, but seldom is the entire hatch lost. The overall population of yearling birds will be down the following spring, but there will still be small entourages of yearling hens that tag along with dominant gobblers throughout the entire season.

Only once, in the spring of 1974, have I seen the woods devoid of yearling turkeys. That was the year following the great 1973 flood, which obliterated every nest in the woods that spring, and persisted so late in the summer that renesting was prevented. During the last two days of the spring season of 1974, Dad and I enjoyed probably the most electrifying turkey hunt we ever had. It was the end of April. All the mature hens had laid full clutches of eggs and had abandoned the gobblers for the season. Unlike in typical seasons, there were no yearling hens, and every gobbler in the woods was completely alone and desperate for affection.

On the first morning, Dad and I parked the Bronco on the Roman Road, and walked together southeast down the road toward Big Bend. We hooted as we walked, but heard no gobbling at first. The river had fallen, and the turkeys had apparently migrated farther inland to Big Bend, feeding along the receding backwater.

When we reached the west edge of the Big Bend area, we heard the first gobble a quarter-mile south of us. Dad went to him, and I continued east for 200 yards, and heard another bird gobbling in the distance.

I took a compass bearing on the bird's location and hurried to him. After 400 steps I reached a good blind-up place, on the contour line where the edge of the backwater had held steady for a while before the river receded.

West of the contour line, above the line where the edge of the water had been, grew normal, lush spring foliage, while on the east side of the line were barren flats where the new growth had been retarded.

Just before reaching that spot, I'd heard two other birds begin to gobble nearby. By the time I finished my blind they were volleying contentiously with the first gobbler on each side of him. I was forced to set up slightly farther from the birds than I wanted, but I couldn't risk moving closer to them because of the stark, open area in front of me.

After finishing the blind, I had only a couple of minutes to call before the gobblers sailed from the roost. I made some soft, short yelps, and cackled twice. As soon as they hit the ground, all three gobblers came to me without hesitation. The first bird apparently was the dominant one because he led the other two.

The dominant gobbler approached quartering to my left, heading to a spot more thickly tangled with vegetation. The lusher foliage screened him from me as he passed by, and he circled around to a spot 70 yards behind me.

The thickness behind me allowed me to turn and move 15 feet to a more strategic location facing him. I carved out two series of solicitous yelps, and got strong gobbles after each. I felt relieved because the gobbler still sounded interested, even anxious.

Later I surmised that the bird reckoned my position incorrectly and missed me as he went by. Most turkeys have an uncanny ability to home in on a sound from remarkable distances, but occasionally one will misread his compass, as that one did. On the few occasions when I've seen it occur, the mistaken bird was an older one whose faculties had perhaps begun to slip a little.

That longbeard was so anxious that, after my last call, he goose-stepped right back to me, and I was able to get him. The bird was indeed an old one. He had above-average-length spurs for our woods, 1-¼ inches.

The other two gobblers were gobbling and almost in range when I shot the first one, and they didn't fly off after the shot. I could have called them up easily had I not decided to leave. All three gobblers had an air of desperation about them, due, I'm sure, to the hen shortage. I neither heard nor saw a hen all morning.

Meanwhile, Dad had checked in at a turkey conclave southwest of me. He heard birds gobbling all around him in every direction for the entire morning. He killed one straight off the roost as I had done, then called up several other gobblers from the same blind, and toyed with them a while. He stayed in the woods until 10:30, which was late for him.

We let the birds rest in the afternoon. The gobblers seemed so vulnerable the first day that we actually felt sorry for them. After discussing it, Dad and I decided to photograph gobblers the next day instead of shooting them.

If your imagination will allow you to picture the Big

Bend area of our woods as being a large convention hotel, you might say that Dad had spent the first morning in the lounge of the hotel, where all the partying was going on. We agreed to return to the lounge together the second morning, and see if the party was still in progress.

The weather the next day was again fair, calm, and beautiful. I don't think that either of us was ever more confident before a turkey hunt than we were that morning. Arrogant might be a better adjective, because we actually walked past the first gobbler we heard and thumbed our noses at him—and he was a hot-gobbling bird within 100 yards of the road we walked on. We passed him by, bent on returning to the same blind Dad had used the previous day.

We didn't hear anything on the roost near Dad's original blind, but we stubbornly sat in it anyway. Soon we began to hear abundant gobbling in every direction, but the gobbling birds were too distant to hear our calling. We stayed put and finally heard a closer one east of us a few minutes later.

When we heard the gobbler, we abandoned the blind and moved in his direction. The scheme was for me to position myself 70 yards in front of Dad in a net-blind with my camera, and he would do the calling from behind me. He started calling while I was setting up the camouflage net, and I had just completed my work and settled to my knees when I detected movement to my left front. Two old longbeards were trotting past me 20 yards to my left, headed directly to Dad.

As quickly as possible without alarming the gobblers, I raised the camera and pressed the shutter release button.

In the tranquil stillness of the divine spring woods, the

*Wade, Sr., after his double-kill with Wade, Jr. in 1974*

faint snap of the camera's shutter sounded like a blacksmith beating out a horseshoe on an anvil. The two gobblers leapt vertically from the ground like mallards leaving a pond, sailed 30 yards past me, and alighted, in a wide-open sprint straight at Dad.

Before the hunt, we'd made a pact that we would not take advantage of the poor, vulnerable turkeys by shooting one. It's peculiar how agreements can be disregarded without a hint of guilt when two broad, swinging beards are coming at you, full steam ahead. I'm disappointed to say Dad couldn't resist the temptation presented him. He threw his box call to the ground, grabbed his Model 12, and fired at the then-veering gobblers. As they flashed by him at top speed, he had difficulty selecting an opening between the trees to shoot through, and he missed them both cleanly.

After the season's roaring finish I called a Ph.D.-type wildlife-biologist friend and discussed the events of the weekend with him. He stated without hesitation that the cause of the gobbler behavior we observed was a lack of hens, including a lack of the usual congregation of yearling hens that normally continue to court gobblers late in the season, after the mature hens all have full clutches of eggs.

I agree with his reasoning completely. I don't remember ever having seen gobblers race around the woods with reckless abandon like that before, and I know it hasn't occurred since then, at least not on Ship Island.

The lone factor distinguishing 1974 from other years was that the preceding year was the only year when we lost 100% of a hatch.

Turkey populations are hard to estimate. We've been incorrect estimating the size of our flock several times. Twice since the 1973 flood, we've endured consecutive years of serious flooding during the nesting and hatching season. On both occasions, the hatches each year appeared to be practically nil because we saw few yearlings during the summer and fall.

When populations on the island did appear to decrease during the two years immediately following the serious floods, both gobbling and hunter success were reduced dramatically, reinforcing our negative conclusions about the floods' effects on the hatches. In those two spring seasons, however, normal hatches returned.

We expected to have only jakes and two-year-old gobblers in the two spring seasons following the return of normal hatches, but, instead, both years we killed three- and four-year-old gobblers almost exclusively.

Some interesting conclusions can be drawn from our post-flood observations. We concluded that the older birds had been present in the first two years of seemingly lower populations after the flood years. During those two years, however, they hadn't gobbled much and few had been harvested, apparently because of heightened awareness.

Another thing that I've observed about floods is that it's easy to underestimate the size of a hatch. In the two instances of consecutive severe floods since 1973, it was obvious later that many more birds hatched on the island during the flood years than we had originally estimated.

We probably experienced below-normal hatches in those years, but they were far from being complete blanks. Populations did decrease later as a result of the floods, but levels were never as low as we had initially estimated.

I don't know where most of the yearlings were in the post-flood years. We observed very few jakes in those years, but they were out there in the woods somewhere. The large number of three- and four-year-old birds taken two and three years later confirmed it.

All of this supports the idea that Mileagris gallopavo is an exceptionally hardy and adaptable species. It has adjusted to severe flooding, loss of habitat, periodic overpopulation of predators, the introduction of new predator species, such as the coyote, into its habitat, and many other threats to its survival.

And it has prospered, even flourished while doing so. The increase from an estimated number of only 4,757 adult birds in Mississippi in 1942, to the current estimate of somewhere between 350,000 and 400,000 birds is a remarkable testimonial to this unique creature. And, of course, much credit should also be given to the Game and Fish personnel who dedicated themselves to the reintroduction and protection efforts which contributed so significantly to this outstanding success story.

## Chapter 19

# Onion Rings and Other Habits

The prophet Isaiah said, "Upon the aged hast thou very heavily laid thy yoke." This proclamation has held true for the original hunters who trod the soil of the old OK Hunting Club in the 1950s. Some, including Dad, have passed on to their reward, and the years are taking their toll on the remainder.

Worn-out knees seem to be the greatest limitation today to the current hunting capabilities of those pioneering hunters on the island. Traversing too many miles to reach distant gobbles, striding over too many logs, leaping from too many boats, and chasing too many half-shot gobblers have combined to tenderize their joints and quench their desire to continue the pursuit of their old bronze-feathered prey.

A new generation hunts the island now, and some are the sons of the pioneers. Roman's son Ted and Dr. Winn's son Hal have continued to hunt there with me. They are two of the original founders of the "Onion-Ring Gang," a subsidiary of the OK Hunting Club, whose members were under 12 years old when it was spun off.

Wild turkey hunting is a trying experience for boys who haven't yet reached their teens. The motivation for us original gang members to come to Tunica was probably 30% turkey hunting and 70% onion rings. The local cafe had the best onion rings anywhere, and, for gang members, a repast there was the climax of the hunt. As we matured, those percentages were more than reversed, and all of us became passionate turkey hunters.

Hal started hunting on Ship Island the same year I did and has honed his turkey-hunting skills to a razor-sharp edge since then. He is one of the most zealous hunters I know.

Hal loves log blinds. I've tried them, but they require a lot of construction time, and I generally lack the patience necessary to build an adequate one. I'm usually anxious to start calling as quickly as possible when I stop to set up.

I suppose Hal acquired a genetic predisposition to build log blinds from his dad, who's built some that look like Fort Laramie. Hal once scuffled around for 45 minutes, accumulating every log in sight, and built a mini-Taj Mahal. A couple of minutes after he had high-jumped over the side of the edifice and sat down, he noticed two cottonmouth-moccasins emerging from under the partially-decomposed bottom-logs, having apparently been dislodged by all the activity. I thought that caper would break Hal of the habit, but the last time I hunted with him he still exhibited a preference for log blinds.

One of Hal's specialties is afternoon turkey hunting. I

love afternoon hunting, too, because I just plain like to spend as much time in the turkey woods as the law allows.

I have a conflict, though. Because of 4:00 a.m. awakenings during turkey season, I enjoy an afternoon nap. Long ago, I decided to accommodate both obsessions, so now on afternoon hunts I frequently lie on my back on a cushioned pad, which facilitates dozing off between series of calls.

Surprisingly, I don't remember even one occasion when my napping prevented me from bagging a gobbler. Of course, ignorance is bliss, and maybe one has walked up 10 steps from me sometime in the past and I slept through it.

Afternoon hunting is often a waiting game, generally with few turkeys seen and little gobbling heard. Wild turkeys seem to be most active in the first hour or so after coming down from the roost, and in the last hour or so before they fly back up. That's not to say that turkeys ever do much running around through the woods, but they definitely seem to move more, and move faster, during those two periods.

When feeding or loafing in the middle of the day, turkeys move about as fast as glaciers, and they can really do a job on a Type-A personality. Despite the frustration, it's fascinating to watch them. They have a way of meandering as they go, like ballet skaters on ice, except much, much slower.

Often they will make no forward progress whatsoever for a period of several minutes, even though they are moving the whole time. I once observed an unusually large (for spring) flock of 22 birds drift by me, grazing like cows in an open section of woods. From 10:15 to 11:45, they moved no more than 100 yards. Smaller groups or single birds often move at about the same pace in midday.

*Hal Winn and Dr. E. H. Winn with a fine double-kill*

These loafing, meandering birds can tie you up in knots sometimes. When some of them turn and take a few steps in your direction, it can put a lump in your throat, because it looks as if they're coming to you. But don't hold your breath. If you wait a minute or two, they'll usually turn and meander a few steps back from where they just came.

The only way to determine which way they're heading is to observe the general direction of their travel over an extended period of time—say, an hour or two. In the case of a dominant gobbler accompanied by a harem of hens, however, you may not even be able to determine where they're going after that long. Sometimes a strutting gobbler and his hens will stay in one spot for several hours without moving so much as 20 yards.

Calling from a blind in the middle of the day may attract birds, even large flocks, but it doesn't necessarily speed them up. For that reason, a hunter has to be prepared to spend some time in the blind if he's convinced he's in an area reasonably well populated with turkeys.

Hunting during midday requires the patience of Job, or better, the patience of someone like Hal Winn. Just when everybody else is tempted to go in and eat a hamburger, Hal's in prime time. There's no telling the number of times I've seen him call up old gobblers at midday and during late afternoon. The book of James says "Let patience have her perfect work." Perfection, of course, can never be attained in the art of wild turkey hunting, but the closest a hunter can come to it is through patience; being willing to wait for as long as it takes.

## Chapter 20

# STREAKERS

Ted Roman, Walter's son, has been coming to Ship Island for more than 25 years. The first time that I realized he had become proficient at the sport of turkey hunting was in a year when the island turkey population was in a downswing.

Ted located a tough gobbler at the head of Earnheartsville Slough one morning and worked him off the roost. He stayed with the recalcitrant longbeard all morning, and the bird finally sauntered off to the southeast in the company of several hens.

It looked like mission impossible for Ted to get the old stud bird to leave those hens, so he tried to plot another strategy. He decided to return early in the afternoon, wait the rest of the day, and try to waylay the old man if he returned to the same roost area.

This strategy sounds remarkably simple. I read in turkey magazines about people doing it all the time. In our river swamps, however, this strategy offers no guarantee of success, because turkeys in the swamp seldom roost in the same trees from day to day, as they seem to in other areas. River-swamp turkeys tend to roost in the same general area, but roost trees often may be 200 yards or more from the previous day's perch. Ted knew this, but he figured that his odds were better trying to do that than trying to lure the emperor away from his concubines again the next morning.

With leafy late-spring foliage, Ted built a blind as thick as a Christmas wreath. From 1:30 to 5, he patiently waited and called with his box call. He didn't overcall. Every 30 minutes or so, he would simply carve out a few yelps and occasionally throw in a single cluck with them.

Ted estimated the birds would fly up to roost at 6:30. If they were indeed headed to a different roost, he knew it would be difficult to call them away from their new roost path to the old one where he was stationed. His confidence began to slip as he considered that possibility.

At 5, Ted became aware of a faint, distant droning sound somewhere behind him. The drone reminded him of when he had been in a sound-proof booth in the doctor's office, taking a hearing exam. The sound he was hearing was similar in a way to the sounds in the booth; the beginning and the end of the sound were both difficult to distinguish. He was only aware of each sound after it had been in progress for a few seconds. "Maybe drumming," he thought. After hearing it several more times, he satisfied himself that it was just that.

The weeds were tall behind him, so he was able to slither down the tree he was leaning against, roll to his stomach, and look to the rear through the branches and leaves of his blind. To his surprise, the drumming gobbler was much nearer than he'd first thought, 25 steps, and was fanned out in a strut, facing away from him.

He waited until the longbeard folded his wings and the long neck became erect, then squeezed the trigger on his three-inch gun and reduced the 19-½ pound gobbler to possession. The bird had never gobbled that afternoon, but Ted was positive that it was the same old gobbler he had been introduced to earlier that morning.

Anybody who hunts turkeys for very long will eventually witness someone get in a hot streak. A man I know fell into one of these streaks on Ashbrook Island 15 years ago. He called up, and shot at, six different groups of long-bearded gobblers over a two-day weekend.

One surprising aspect of the hunt was that the man was a relatively neophyte turkey hunter. His inexperience showed, because in spite of having that many shots, he brought not a single turkey back to camp with him. Further, I seem to remember that he didn't even find a single feather dislodged from a bird.

Another surprising aspect about that streak demonstrates how perplexing turkey hunting can be. The club member who hosted the inept shooter, and everyone else in the camp, had been hunting wild turkeys since as early as World War II, and they never saw a turkey the entire weekend.

The guest hunted in several different locations on the island during the two-day hunt, and no matter where he went, a light brigade of gobblers would charge his blind only minutes after his first feeble yelps. Like Midas, everything he touched turned to gold.

I have occasionally experienced the good fortune of getting in the way of a hot streak. One of my more memorable ones occurred in the spring of 1981, when I set up in four separate locations, from Big Bend to the Slash, between daylight and 10:15, and called one or more longbeards into shotgun range at each location. Of course, I didn't take a shot each time.

One of the better hot streaks on Ship Island occurred over two short hunts in consecutive spring seasons, and it happened to Ted Roman. Ted lives in Alabama now, and makes only one trip to the island each year.

On the first trip, Ted climbed into a high deer stand in Earnheartsville the first morning so he could hear better. A distant gobbler answered a yelp made on the box call he'd purchased just before the trip.

Ted had no faith that the gobbler would seriously consider approaching the sound of a hen originating 15 feet in the air at midmorning, so he climbed down and set up again. Only minutes after he had moved, a four-year-old gobbler walked into range, and Ted leveled him.

On the second day's hunt, Ted went to a completely different area and killed a two-year-old gobbler in the afternoon. The bird walked up to him only 25 minutes after he sat down to call.

On the third day's hunt, Ted heard a bird gobble on the roost only 200 yards from where he stopped his Jeep, and he proceeded to have one of those classic "slam, bam, thank you ma'am" hunts.

He sauntered over, sat down, called only once on his magic box, and had a gobbler pitch down practically into his lap. The only variation on this hunt was that the thought of killing three in a row psyched Ted out so much that he missed the bird.

Ted had such a hot hand that he probably could have sat in a blind on top of the levee, called once on his box, and had a gobbler fly 600 yards and alight in the gravel road. I thought he would cool down some in the off season, but when he returned the next spring, he was still smoking.

I was in the woods hunting when he rolled in from Alabama one afternoon the next year. Since he would be arriving late and would have limited hunting time that first day, we had agreed that the best place for him to hunt would be the Red Line area because it was easily and quickly accessible.

I should have predicted that Ted wouldn't need a lot of time. When he reached the island a little before dark, he parked on the dirt road, and changed from his three-piece suit into his camouflage. Then he walked about 300 yards, sat down just off the Red Line Road, and called a couple of times on the same magic box he had debuted a year earlier.

I never heard a shot, because I was hunting the south end. When I met Ted at the gate at dark, he had already changed into slacks and dress shirt in preparation for eating onion rings at the Blue & White cafe in town. He opened the rear gate on his Jeep and matter-of-factly showed me a monstrous, still-warm gobbler.

He proceeded to call up and kill another big gobbler the next morning, and after he began to feel a few pangs of guilt, he called up one more the second morning for his father.

Ted's success lends credence to a theory to which I've heard several hunters subscribe: that the introduction of a completely new-sounding call, or method of calling, to an area often is met with a surprisingly good response from the residents.

*Ted Roman with one of the gobblers taken during his hot streak*

All of us on Ship Island had primarily used almost-identical extra-raspy box calls prior to Ted's arrival, and the turkeys had probably become a little call-shy to that type of call. When the turkeys heard the smoother, purer tone of Ted's new box call, they just couldn't resist bopping over to check out the new dame in town.

## Chapter 21

# WALKING THE TALK

For the past few spring turkey seasons, I've hunted a hilly area in Franklin County, Mississippi, on opening day. Franklin County is about 250 miles south of Tunica County, and the gobbling in Franklin County seems to run about 10 days earlier.

Gobbling is nil to minimal on opening day in Tunica County, but I've heard as many as six or seven gobblers gobbling, and gobbling a lot, on opening day in Franklin County.

I always enjoy hunting in Franklin County, because it's such a contrast to Delta swamp hunting. The difference lies mostly in the topographical dissimilarities between the two areas.

Because of flat terrain in the Mississippi River bottomlands, you can't move easily on a turkey that you're working. Unless the woods have been cut over heavily, which encourages lusher growth of understory vegetation, the flat terrain makes a hunter's movements much more visible to turkeys.

The most common situation where movement can be helpful is when an old gobbler that you've been working decides the hen (which is actually you) is not coming to him, and he moves off through the woods. A hill hunter may be able to move when a gobbler is only 40 yards away, because the bird may go into a ravine or over a rise. Ridges, ravines, creek bottoms, and other terrain features in the hill country facilitate movement there. Even gradual elevation changes can frequently screen a hunter's movement. Typically though, the swamp hunter has to stay put and try all his calling tricks until the bird moves far enough away to allow movement, which is frequently a distance of 200 yards or more. Moving on a bird is usually more successful when you can make your move before the gobbler puts that much distance between you and him.

Movement is a valuable weapon in a hunter's arsenal because of the realism it adds to the caller's attempt to behave and sound like a real hen. The next time you're surrounded by hens, pay attention to what they do when you hear them calling. You'll quickly notice that real hens are almost always moving, maybe slowly, but moving.

Usually you can tell by the movement associated with it whether the calling you hear is made by a hunter or a hen. I have observed this while hunting on public or crowded private forestland. If you hear hen-calling originating from the same location for a prolonged period, say 15 minutes or more, it's almost certainly calling made by another hunter.

This rule does not apply to gobbling, however. Old hung-up gobblers often continue to gobble from the same spot for long periods, as do gobblers that are trying to call hens to their strut zones.

I first learned the value of moving while calling about 25 years ago, while hunting at Ship Island with Willie Green and a now-deceased friend, Buddy Gibson.

We all separated at daylight and dispersed into three separate areas to hunt.

I was hunting Big Bend and Buddy was on the ridge east of the Slash. We had agreed beforehand that the Log Dump Road would be the line separating our respective hunting areas.

I didn't hear any gobbling or have any luck early. Later, I was walking back to the Bronco on the Log Dump Road, yelping every 200 steps as I went. Immediately after one of my calls I heard a gobbler, as Ben Lee used to say, "cut" my yelps with a gobble before they were finished.

The gobble came from west of the road, 150 yards inside Buddy's territory. The yelp apparently jump-started the gobbler, and he began to gobble every 30 seconds or so.

I stood and simply listened to the gobbler for a few minutes. I didn't hear any hen calls in that direction, so my first thought was that Buddy was over by the Slash and wasn't working the turkey.

It was late in the spring, and the woods were sufficiently greened-up to allow me to move closer to the bird for a setup. Nevertheless, Ship Island etiquette mandated that I stay out of my partner's territory.

I decided that if I couldn't move to the bird, I would do the next-best thing. I sat down against a tree on my side of the road and listened for several more minutes to make sure I didn't hear Buddy calling. When I didn't, I made a couple of calls and got robust responses from the gobbler. The bird was hung up and didn't budge, but he continued to gobble well for 30 minutes.

I hadn't built a blind, and I suddenly realized that I had to hide better if I was to have a chance with the bird. I waited until I heard the bird's next gobble, to make sure he wasn't moving toward me, then got up and moved 50 feet down the road away from him to a natural blind I had seen.

As soon as I reached the blind, I called and my yelps were again "cut" by his responding gobble. A minute later his gobble was closer. He was rapidly approaching me.

As gobblers so often do when they make their final approach, the bronze wonder became silent. We had logged only two years before, and the tops from the logging job, combined with the profuse, late spring understory, made the woods dense in the area. I couldn't see the gobbler approaching and, if he came, I was unsure where he would step from the foliage and cross the road.

He was stepping like Groucho Marx when he emerged, and his thick old beard was like an umpire's brush dusting the road when he crossed it 18 yards to my left. I was forced to turn to shoot as he passed by. I would like to offer that as my excuse for missing him clean, but it's admittedly a weak one.

I always feel the same when I miss a turkey. It's one of the sickest feelings I know. I realize a rare opportunity has been squandered, and I hate most the thought that I may have crippled a beautiful bird and sent him on his way suffering.

When I miss a gobbler, I always mentally replay the sequence dozens of times, and I seldom find a good solid reason for the miss. My conclusion in that case was that my pattern was small at 18 steps and I must have shot high. I did that several times until I decided to have a midbarrel bead installed on my gun.

After my shot sequence, I heard Buddy yelling from out in the woods across the road. I yelled back for locational purposes, and when he reached me he told his story.

He had located the big gobbler on the roost and had been working him ever since. He tried every call in his possession, and he had a coat full of them, because he was one of those hill boys.

The bird hung up on Buddy, and he couldn't move around because he was in a relatively open spot. When he heard me begin calling, he heard the gobbler move away from him.

I bask in no self-glory at the thought of how I "called that gobbler off Buddy" that morning. Even then, I had been hunting long enough to know better; my calling sounded no better than his.

I was convinced then, and still am, that the burly bird was pulled away by the illusion of a brand-new "hen" entering his area, and by the realism that the "hen's" movement added to the situation.

Since that day, I have tried to incorporate movement into my hunting as much as possible, but I haven't been as successful as I would like, due to our open swamps. At our latitude, the woods are seldom greened-up enough to allow much movement before the last two weeks of the spring season. Even then, we have to be careful, because those suspicious little eyes are always out there scrutinizing every twitch.

## Chapter 22

# SITTERS VS. WALKERS

Some of the hardest times for turkey hunters are those occasions, usually in midday, when the gobblers aren't gobbling and all the turkeys appear to be in hiding. My father's reasoning for this phenomenon was that a designated turkey blew a whistle at noon somewhere in the woods, and all the turkeys simultaneously screwed themselves into the ground and completely disappeared.

Whatever the reason, turkeys can often be extremely difficult to locate at midday. It can be quite a letdown for a hunter after he's heard perhaps dozens of gobbles and seen lots of activity earlier the same day. A hunter usually must change tactics to have success at midday.

Most experienced hunters in our region assume either of two identities in those generally stagnated hours of midday; they either become "walkers" or "sitters."

Walkers like to cover as much area as possible, calling every 100 or 200 steps, hoping to solicit a gobble from a rambunctious longbeard.

Sitters tend to be extremely patient types, who are capable of remaining motionless in the same blind for hours on end, even when they haven't seen any birds or heard any turkey talk.

Walkers are usually the more disliked of the two types. I don't recall ever hearing a walker slander a sitter, but I've heard sitters cuss walkers on many occasions.

If put to the question, I would have to describe myself as being in the gray area between the two philosophies. One of the aspects of spring hunting at Ship Island's latitude is that the season is usually half over before the woods leaf out significantly. During the first half of the season, it's not difficult to see a moving object through the woods at least 200 yards away.

Because I detest the thought of unnecessarily enhancing the anxious temperament of wild turkeys, I almost always sit still during the first half of the season. I move under the cover of predawn darkness to my calling location, and generally stay put until I terminate my hunt. To avoid being spotted by birds during daylight hours, I also use the densest corridors of the woods as routes of egress.

During the second half of the season, however, I don't hesitate to walk if I feel it's indicated. The woods then are much thicker, and generally prevent the detection of a moving hunter more than 40 or 50 yards away.

Some would probably argue with me, but I feel that, in thicker woods in the late spring, a walker probably has the odds on his side. Generally, his calling will be heard by more eligible gobblers, because he'll cover a larger area.

Twenty years ago, I used mouth calls almost exclusively

while walking, primarily for the sake of convenience. Now, I use a homemade, solid-walnut box call most of the time, because it has more volume and it broadcasts sound to a wider area.

Numerous positive experiences using the walking technique have reinforced my confidence in it. One of these occurred on a windy, late-season day in the 1976 spring season. Having had no luck earlier, I decided at midmorning to start walking and calling with a diaphragm mouth caller.

I usually call every 200 steps while walking, but due to high winds, I was calling more frequently that day. At 9:30, after 30 minutes of moving, I was surprised by a strong gobble only 75 yards east of the Log Dump Road.

I knew that a proximate gobbler answering me that late in the morning could be on top of me in a flash, so I simply knelt in the shade of a hackberry tree beside the road.

Within three minutes I spotted the approaching ashen head, visible only a couple of inches above the tops of the tall poison ivy stems. I was able to raise my shotgun when his head briefly dipped below the weeds, and I shot the three-year-old gobbler at 22 steps as he was steadily marching to me. After the shot, several hens flew off from behind him.

As an aside to this story, when I cleaned the gobbler later, I found that his crop was stretched tight with peanuts, which were fresh enough to have been eaten since he flew off the roost earlier the same morning. I knew there were no peanuts planted anywhere in our woods, so I began to ask around town about it. I discovered that peanuts had been planted in a field south of us, on another hunting club. On my aerial photograph, I scaled the distance from the peanut field to the spot where I had killed the turkey, and found it to be a mile and a half.

I'm not aware of a dominant gobbler and a harem of hens ever ranging that far in such a short period of time in our woods before, especially during the mating season, when they usually stay within an area of perhaps only 100 acres or so. The only logical conclusion I could draw from it was that the whole flock had been spooked and flushed from the feeding area earlier that morning, after having had time enough to fly off the roost and stuff themselves.

It was also unusual to see evidence of a dominant gobbler eating that much so early in the morning during the prime mating season. In the spring, dominant gobblers typically are much more concerned with servicing hens than they are with dining. I've seen many dominant gobblers cleaned and plucked in the spring, and most of them had little, or nothing at all, in their crops, even if they were taken in late afternoon.

Getting back to the walking method, it does admittedly have three possible disadvantages. One is that a silent gobbler will occasionally be run away by a hunter's movement through the woods. Thicker late-season foliage, however, usually minimizes such an occurrence, and often a silent bird nearby won't detect the stalking hunter, especially if he is walking silently on a road.

Some hunters worry about missing these silent gobblers, and they prefer to wait a while after pausing to make each call. They usually stop every 400 yards or so, set up, and call for about 20 minutes before moving on.

This method has never particularly appealed to me,

*The author with The "Peanut Gobbler"*

because it slows me down and limits the area I cover and the number of gobblers that might hear me.

Certainly some gobblers that might otherwise be workable will be passed-up by the hunter who walks until he elicits a gobble. If probabilities are considered, however, the odds of working a bird are probably better if the hunter maximizes his area of coverage.

A second disadvantage is that a walking hunter sometimes may cover miles before he makes contact with an agreeable gobbler, or he may walk miles and never encounter anything at all. At least, however, he can feel secure in knowing that his conditioning has improved.

The third disadvantage of walking and calling is a more serious one. Calling while moving through woods can be hazardous to your health, if it's done in territory where the reliability and experience level of the other hunters is unknown.

I found this out for myself. I was shot once when I was calling and walking through woods frequented by unfamiliar hunters. One thing that helped me was that the shooter was 49 steps from me, beyond good range for a 12 gauge, three-inch magnum, shooting No. 6 shot. But The Lord had to be watching out for me, too. Several pellets penetrated my face and neck, but they failed to strike arteries or anything else vital.

I am abundantly cautious now about where I hunt and with whom I hunt. And, even in my own woods, I often wear a blaze-orange cap and vest when traveling in the woods. When I hunt in public areas, I also pin the vest on the back side of my tree with push-pins when I set up.

Some of my friends prefer sitting to walking. Hal Winn is one of them. I'm not quite sure how Hal does it, but he can sit in a blind in quiet woods at midday and call up respectable gobblers surprisingly often.

One such time was in 1982 at Ship Island. I was escorting someone to another area, and dropped Hal off in Earnheartsville on the way. He entered the woods, and at the first signs of fresh scratching, he stopped and decided to construct a log blind just high enough to screen him while he lay in a prone position.

Hal lay on his back and commenced calling on his favorite Stribling box call. The box is a loud one, and Hal blasted the southern end of Earnheartsville with it that afternoon, carving out staccato yelps, cutts, and cackles.

He lay there performing his calling routine for a solid two hours without hearing a single turkey respond, and without seeing anything more significant than a chickadee. He was tenacious, however, and decided that he was going to shack up with the turkeys for the whole afternoon.

Hal's patience usually rewards him. It did again that afternoon, because he soon detected movement north of his low blind. Two huge, long-whiskered birds were quartering through the woods 90 yards in front of him.

Because they weren't headed directly toward his blind, Hal wasn't sure whether they were simply traveling through the area, or if they were attempting to locate him and had incorrectly coursed the sounds of his calling.

Many hunters cease calling when a gobbler appears at moderate range, hoping that the bird is already zeroed in on the sound. Hal, though, is not bashful in such situations. He often continues calling until the gobbler walks up close.

Hal kept petitioning the two husky gobblers with his Stribling box, and succeeded in turning them his way. They both lumbered over to him and Hal knocked down the larger one with his old Model 12.

Hal's successful hunt also illustrates an important element of productive turkey calling that is utilized by good callers: that it's best to call as loud as you can when you're not on a gobbler and you're simply prospecting for an interested bird.

Everyone knows that it's often important to call softly when a gobbler is close, but when it's midday and nothing is happening, louder is generally better. That's one reason my buddy John Eddleman and I like to make box calls out of solid blocks of dense hardwood, like walnut or persimmon. Not only are these boxes extremely raspy; they're the loudest we've ever heard. They are just the thing for eliciting distant shock-gobbles in the middle of an otherwise dull day, whether you call yourself a sitter or a walker.

## Chapter 23

# GOBBLER CALLS ARE FOR THE BIRDS

Novice turkey hunters are usually instructed to try to trick gobblers by acting like surrogate hens. Most soon discover, however, that often something more than plain yelps and clucks is needed in order to tempt most gobblers into shotgun range. Sometimes a hunter needs to emulate a competing courter rather than a lover, and make a few gobbles.

I approach this subject with caution. Although it wasn't caused by my gobbling, I was once shot while turkey hunting, and I'm of the opinion that nothing else places a hunter in more peril than to imitate gobbling.

When I first started turkey hunting in the late 1950s, there were few turkey calls, hunting clothes, and other turkey-hunting gear available for purchase. The mouth-diaphragm call had only recently been invented but wasn't commercially available in my hometown.

There was no National Wild Turkey Federation then. It was born in 1973. There were no magazines and almost no books available on the subject of turkey hunting. Little how-to information existed in print form. The chief source of information on what to do and how to do it was the "old timer."

All the old timers said, "Never gobble." The common logic of the day dictated that since gobblers were looking for hens, gobble-calls, and even gobbler yelps and clucks, would run your bird off.

Never mind that Lynch boxes were made with the words "hen side" stamped on one side and the words "gobbler side" stamped on the other. I don't remember anyone questioning why that was. I suppose everyone just figured the gobbler side was put there as a novelty.

The gobbler side of a box call always intrigued me. After a few years of contemplation, I finally started experimenting with imitating gobbles in the woods. I basically learned by trial and error that a gobble call does have some value as an additional tool in the hunter's bag.

Gobbling comes in only two forms that I know of: the full-blown gobbling of an old mature gobbler and jake-gobbling, which has an element of finesse in it.

Listen to jakes in the woods. Fall jakes are seldom able to gobble, but I've heard them trying, and it's one of the most humorous and entertaining sounds you'll hear in the woods. They usually start their gobbles off with yelps and sound something like this: "yelp... yelp... yelp.. yelp.yelp.yelp-yonk." The yonk at the end is lower pitched than the yelps, and appears to be the jake's juvenile-ish attempt to initiate a gobble.

By the following spring, some jakes will actually be able to gobble, but a trained ear usually can distinguish them from adult gobblers. A lot of these year-old gobblers continue to initiate their gobbles with two or three yelps. A few are able to gobble without the introductory yelps, but even they are generally distinguishable from adults by the brevity of their gobbles.

Only occasionally will a jake be polished enough to fool an experienced ear. Even those that are able to realistically imitate an adult usually cannot do it every time they try. They often slip or voluntarily revert to childhood habits, between their more-refined gobbles.

I've discovered the jake gobble to be more useful than the adult gobble because it has the intended effect on a wider audience. Remember that, in the spring, male turkeys are in fight mode. Adult gobblers are busy trying to assert territorial rights, which are basically the rights to every hen within the territory.

It stands to reason, however, that there are more gobblers, both juvenile and adult, that are unsuccessful at dominating a territory than there are those who can do the dominating. Before we hunters enter the woods on opening day of the spring season, many fights have already occurred, and most of the gobblers have learned the hard way their rank in the pecking order.

I had been experimenting with a jake gobble for several years before I really began to appreciate its value as a call. I had developed a reasonably decent facsimile of one with a box call, but I wasn't having the results I'd hoped for.

I decided to try a snuff-can caller one spring. I didn't like the yelps and clucks it made, but I was able to generate a convincing imitation of a gobble on it. The call's instructional-tape-quality gobbles more than offset the mediocre introductory jake-yelps it made. I started carrying it to the woods with me solely for the purpose of making gobbles.

The first field test of my new discovery occurred on an early spring hunt with Willard McIlwain at Ship Island. The weekend got off to an adverse start when we had our sleep disrupted at the aging local motel the night before, and were forced to go the woods in sluggish condition.

I was the first one to awaken in the night, aroused by a series of light sounds that I discerned to be emanating from the bathroom. Each was a two-note series repeated in the same sequence: bap..thud, bap..thud, bap..thud.

I'd noticed the night before that the crank handles on the casement windows in the bathroom were corroded sufficiently to prevent the windows from closing. As my hazy mind slowly awakened, my initial thought was that an intruder had broken into our bathroom.

McIlwain awakened shortly after I did, and we discussed the situation in hushed whispers. I remembered that my shotgun was standing in a corner, so I eased out of bed as quickly as possible and quietly slipped a shell in the chamber. I tiptoed to the door at port arms and cautiously peeked around the corner into the bathroom.

The bathroom light had been left on when we retired for the night, but, even with its illumination, I was unable to see anything when I looked around the corner. Although the frequency of the strange noises was decreasing, I could still hear them coming from somewhere in the bathroom.

I studied the room and finally realized the sounds were

originating in the trash can below the sink. Stepping cautiously forward, I looked inside the can and the mystery was solved.

Inside the can was a hyperventilating mouse, nearly exhausted from five endless minutes of frantic high-jumping. The alarming sounds were the baps of the leaping mouse striking the side of the plastic can, followed by thuds as he fell back down to the bottom.

I promptly seized the can, marched to the front door, and catapulted the contents of the can into the gravel parking lot. The terrified rodent hit the ground with four legs flailing, and I watched in stunned disbelief as it streaked straight back between my legs. He was inside our room before I could react, and I was forced to endure the sound of McIlwain's unbridled laughter while I searched under the beds for the creature.

The search was in vain. The mouse had vanished, and we were compelled to return to our beds without knowing his exact whereabouts in the room.

Sleep never returned before the alarm went off. We lay in our beds the remainder of the night expecting at any moment to feel tiny paws treading across our backs.

The river was up and we had to boat to our destinations the next morning. I dropped McIlwain in Earnheartsville and continued in the boat to the Roman Road Ridge.

I was walking on the Roman Road when I heard two gobblers crank up over the flooded slough north of me. I set up on them and made two or three series of soft yelps on both my box call and a mouth call. One of the gobblers sailed off the roost at 5:35, alighted 80 steps from me, and walked northwest away from me, along the edge of the slough. As he moved away, the second gobbler pitched to the ridge and joined him.

Seeing no hens with the two birds, and thinking they were probably subordinate birds, I made a couple of series of gobbler yelps, hoping they would want to join up with another subordinate. With this, both of them turned and started scratching back my way along the water's edge.

When they were 60 steps away, they veered and began to loop around me, barely out of range. After an hour and fifteen minutes, they had passed and fed off out of sight behind me.

Out of frustration, I shifted to the other side of my tree and made two series of jake gobbles on my untested snuff-can caller. There was no response, but after two minutes I glimpsed both gobblers moving toward me. They trotted right up without stopping, and I had to shoot the leader at 13 steps to keep him from trampling me.

I was delighted with the initial performance of my new secret weapon. Rookie successes often turn to sophomore swoons, however, and that proved to be the case with the new call. Before the end of that same spring season, I found that it was not infallible. It didn't work every time out.

That's so often the case in turkey hunting. Nothing works every time. Occasionally, I'll find some new technique, or new caller, or way of calling, and it will seem to work unbelievably well two or three times in a row. I'll begin to think that I've finally found that magic call, that missing link to astounding turkey-hunting success that we all seek.

I've been tempted several times by some new discovery

to fall into the trap of thinking this way. I've been disappointed each time, however, and by now I've become calloused about it because I realize there's no such thing. If something worked every time, we wouldn't be as consumed with our sport as we are.

Nevertheless, the jake-gobble has been a valuable addition to my repertoire, especially when produced with a snuff-can or other tube-type caller. I've used the call to lure numerous birds that refused to come to other calls.

The full-blown gobble of a mature gobbler also has considerable merit as a call. I advise caution when you use it, however, because it may scare away some gobblers. Since most of the gobbler population in a given area is comprised of subdominant males, it's logical that adult-gobbles will raise the suspicions of more birds than will jake-gobbles. No self-respecting male two-years-old or older feels threatened by a yearling.

I only use a full gobble when I'm reasonably certain that my quarry is a dominant gobbler. This is not always easy to determine, however. A gobbler's tendency to hang up is one indicator of dominance, but it's not absolute. Be alert to the sight or sounds of hens with the gobbler. The presence of hens is probably the best indicator of dominance.

I've had more success using a full gobble when I've used it later in the game, after an hour or more of using other hen calls. The longer you wait, the better chance you have to judge dominance by hearing or seeing hens. And, the longer you wait, the better you can set the bird up for using the gobble.

Once when I was hunting with my son Bob, I worked a

tough bird for 3-½ hours before finally getting him into shotgun range. He was a classic bird. I tried every play in my playbook that morning, but it was only after four hens came from his direction and walked right by us that I began using full-blown gobbles. The hens confirmed to me that he was a dominant bird. Even after I started using the gobbles, it took about an hour-and-a-half to get the gobbler up to us.

It's hard to predict how fast a given gobbler will come in response to a gobble. I've had them come up immediately, but I've also seen them take a long time to come. Sometimes, they'll come up trotting or walking fast, red-headed and ready to brawl. But, sometimes they'll come up slow, and even stop and strut along the way.

I suppose the difference in response time is caused simply by differences in the individual personalities of the turkeys, or by the presence of hens. Whatever the cause, ain't it great that we have such daily variety in our experiences with this magnificent game bird?

## Chapter 24

# HE HAD A FIELD DAY

John Eddleman will probably tell you that his greatest turkey hunting experience occurred late one spring season when he was on a two-day hunt at Ship Island. That spring, the turkeys seemed to cycle out of their breeding behavior patterns earlier than usual. Gobbling had tapered off substantially, and the birds seemed to be more interested in feeding than in mating.

I was unable to locate any gobbling birds on the first of the two mornings we went out, but Eddleman located a big gobbler escorting eight hens out in a field, and thus began possibly the most entertaining two days of his life.

Field hunting is a privilege almost exclusively enjoyed by the hill boys. I read about field hunting and field-hunting strategies primarily in books authored by hill hunters, such as Gene Nunnery, Jack Dudley, and others, and in national magazine articles.

Field hunting is something we deep-woods hunters in the Mississippi River Delta floodplain seldom get to experience. In the first place, most of our timber tracts are on the unprotected side of the river levee, where flood risk limits agricultural practices. Most of the fields there are large "sand-blow" fields, where sand deposits from past floods are so deep that most trees won't grow. There are a few fields with decent soil types, but most of them are used for row crops.

In most cases, fields of either of the above two types are usually large; in many cases, several hundred acres in size. Fields that big don't have the cozy feel of a small pasture set in the middle of a tract of pine and upland hardwood in the hills. They generally don't allow a hunter to develop a close relationship with a turkey like the smaller fields do.

Variation in distance is probably the reason for this. A square, 20-acre field or pasture, which would probably be of above-average size in the middle of a forested hill tract, is 933 feet on a side. A gobbler standing in the middle of the 20-acre field is half that distance, or 467 feet, from any side of the field. That is only 156 yards, a common distance from which turkeys are called by hunters in deep woods.

Consider, however, a 200-acre field, which is closer to typical size for fields on most Mississippi River hunting clubs. A square, 200-acre field has 2,952-foot sides. A turkey in the middle of a field this size would be 1,476 feet, or more than a quarter of a mile, from any side of the field. A turkey there might not even hear a hunter calling, especially if a breeze is blowing against the hunter. Even if the bird does hear the calling, he would likely not respond as well as he would from the middle of a smaller field. Many fields are not square, of course, but this size principle is still important, even in large fields with irregular sides.

Along the river, turkeys are more inclined to use fields on two occasions. One is when the mosquitos are at their worst. Turkeys will take refuge in a field then, because the breeze is stronger there and tends to keep the mosquitos at bay.

Another occasion is late in the spring season, when hens begin to nest. Many hens prefer to nest around field edges because the poults that hatch later will be able to find more bugs there, and often the edges are thicker. Eddleman's celebrated hunt occurred late in the spring, when nesting was in full swing.

John began his hunt that morning in the woods south of the 22-acre South Cottonwood Field, which is located north of Paw Paw Ridge in Bailey's Woods. He'd heard no roost gobbling early, but shortly after fly-down time he was scouting farther east, and heard a gobbler on the ground crank up.

As he approached the bird, he discovered that it was in the field. He crept cautiously through thick cane along the edge of the field until he reached a place in the southwest corner where he could peer out. He saw the gobbler standing in a full strut only 50 steps from the edge, with eight hens slowly pecking around him, like wagons circled in an indian attack. John didn't realize then that he would not be that close to the gobbler again for 24 more hours.

Following suggestions he'd seen in magazine articles, Eddleman made a blind in the edge of the woods, placed his hen decoy near the field, and began to call to the old waddled-and-whiskered curmudgeon. The huge bird responded without hesitation to every call John made, but approached not one step closer to the woods line.

After a short time, the entire entourage moved out until they reached the middle of the field, 300 yards away. There they milled around for the remainder of the morning. John continued to call periodically, even mixing a few gobbles in, but to no avail.

At noon, with the birds still in middle of the field, Eddleman's appetite persuaded him to depart and meet Dr. Winn and me back at camp. After a light repast, he returned to the same blind on the edge of the field to view the drama that had so entertained him earlier. As he expected, when he returned all was status quo in the field. The birds had moved scarcely 20 feet from where they had been.

As soon as John had plopped onto his foam cushion, he resumed calling, this time folding more gobbles into the mix. After an hour, the hens began to drift his way, slowly ambling to within 30 yards of him before returning to the strutting gobbler in the center of the field.

The birds remained there for the rest of the afternoon. Just before dusk they moved south to the woods where they would roost, cruising past John only 70 steps from the edge of the field. All Eddleman could discuss that evening was the lascivious boss gobbler and his mistresses in the field, and the tactical options available to lure them the following morning.

Despite a night of tossing and turning, Eddleman leapt out of bed like a leprechaun at four the next morning.

John's best guess was that the birds had roosted somewhere down on Paw Paw Ridge, south of the field. Based on this assumption, he planned to walk from the north to the south end of the field under cover of darkness, intending to set up on the edge there. His hope was to be near enough to the gobbler's path to be able to cut him off as he headed back into the field.

As John walked through the field, distant barred-owl hoots stirred the stud gobbler to assert his initial proclamation of the day. John was shocked to hear his gobble originate from the identical spot from which he had called the afternoon before. He wondered how it had been possible to leave the night before without disturbing the roosting bird.

When John reached the woods at the south end he set up a blind there, within 150 steps of the gobbler roosted off the southwest corner. This time, he sat his decoy in the field, and began calling softly.

As the sky gathered a peach-tinted hue, the boss began to gobble confidently and often. His gobbles totalled 15 or 20 before he departed his tree. As John watched from his blind, the old boy and the eight hens sailed directly from their cottonwood perches into the field. Upon alighting, the longbeard immediately resumed a strut pose.

At first, the gobbler seemed inclined to leave the hens. He began to stroll toward the decoy stationed in the field 20 yards from John. A lump began to arise in John's throat.

The gobbler soon pivoted, however, rejoined the hens, and escorted them to the middle of the field again, in spite of John's increasingly desperate cackling and gobbling.

It appeared to John that the stage was set for a repeat of the previous day's events, another 12 hours of simply observing wild turkey behavior, like a wildlife biologist conducting research for his doctoral dissertation.

The winds of fortune soon shifted, though, and began

to waft Eddleman's way. Two things would prevent the morning from being routine. The first occurred only a few minutes after the turkeys reached the middle of the field, 300 yards away.

As he sat there observing the flock, Eddleman's eyes detected the movement of a new object in the northwest corner of the field, the same corner through which he had entered the field an hour earlier under cover of darkness. He squinted to identify the slow-moving, pale-yellow object, 500 yards distant. It was a medium-sized dog.

Either by design or by chance, the dog appeared to be trotting straight toward the hens, which were meandering 40 steps from where their whiskered master stood.

When the gobbler observed the dog approaching the hens, you couldn't have made the burly old bird any madder had you kicked his tail feathers. His rage provoked him into doing one of the most unique and comical things I've ever heard of: In full strut, he charged across the field toward the dismayed mutt, gobbling at him the whole way.

Despite a considerable weight advantage, the dog was completely intimidated, and it broke and ran out of the field the way it had entered.

After the gobbler had chased the impudent stray from his domain, he sauntered back to the vicinity of his harem, still fanned out in a pompous display of vanity.

When John saw the gobbler return to the hens, he decided to resume calling aggressively. He cackled, cutt, gobbled, and jake-gobbled almost constantly for the next 10 minutes.

The longbeard continued to answer him well, but moved no closer. Then, at 8:30, the second uncommon occurrence of the morning began to evolve.

From the woods behind John, three jakes slowly fed by, entered the field, and passed within 15 yards of the decoy. Playfully, John began cutting at them.

His calling initiated a frenzy of cutting from the jakes in response. John became absorbed in their antics, and didn't notice until a couple of minutes later that the stud had begun moving in his direction.

When John diverted his gaze back to the master gobbler, he saw the bird enroute, still in a full strut. The gobbler looked almost comical in the way he attempted to trot, with all his feathers starched out. When he quartered slightly sideways in his approach, his wings obscured his moving legs, and he appeared to be floating, like a round puff of dark smoke adrift on a soft breeze.

As Eddleman held his breath, the boss pulled on his reins and halted 50 yards from the woods line, giving his pursuing hens a chance to overtake him. When the hens had joined him, they all quartered across to the tree line in the southeast corner of the field where they were far to John's right and out of his view.

From there, John expected them to enter the woods, so he started calling softer, with hen yelps only.

A few minutes later, he spied the gobbler returning from the corner, quartering across the field again in front of him. His path would place him nearer to Eddleman's position than he had been on either day. John concluded that if the bird passed by anywhere near the range limit of his shotgun, he would take the shot.

John estimated there would only be one point where the crossing gobbler's path would be tangent to the effective range limit of his gun. He didn't feel secure, however, because he was aware of the difficulty in estimating distances in an open field.

Luckily, the gobbler stayed on course, and when the bird reached the predetermined point, John squeezed off a shot. As the gobbler staggered back, John thought he heard the secondary sound of shot slamming into the bird's feathers.

It worried him because he knew that the sound of pellets hitting a bird can only be heard on long shots. The fleeting thought flashed through his mind that he might have underestimated the distance and had only crippled the handsome bird.

After the gobbler staggered, it appeared for a moment that he might regain enough strength to escape, but then he collapsed into terminal convulsions of flopping. Eddleman counted 43 paces to the bird, about six steps beyond his comfort range.

I met John an hour later, and he enthusiastically recounted the tale to me. Cumulatively, he had hunted this gobbler of his dreams for 12 hours over the two-day period. The gobbler had answered almost every call he had made during the period, and was in a full-blown strut for approximately 10 of the 12 hours. He had a field day, all right—a field two days, in fact. Now, when Eddleman doesn't show up back at the vehicle at the appointed time after a hunt, I know where to look for him. I just drive the fields on the north end, and I usually find him along the edge somewhere, with his eyes gazing far off in the distance, wishing he could turn back the hands of time.

## Chapter 25

# EAST OF THE SLASH

I know a wealthy gentleman whose wife once commissioned an artist to paint on canvas his favorite pond at his duck-hunting club for a Christmas present. I first saw this painting at least 25 years ago, and ever since then, I've dreamed of hanging paintings of my favorite Ship Island turkey ridges on my den wall.

Such a thing is unlikely to happen, though, not only because of the expense, but also because I don't think I could find an artist who would be willing to hike a mile through bull nettle and mosquitos to paint them for me.

Some places on the island are so special to me that I've even considered telling my family to lay me to rest at one of them when the time comes. I suppose the reason I haven't done it is because I'm concerned that it might unnecessarily inconvenience the mourners.

It's trouble enough for folks to attend a funeral downtown, much less one in a swamp. It wouldn't be easy for the funeral director either. I don't believe he'd have access to a four-wheel-drive Cadillac hearse.

All this aside, there are many places on the island that I cherish. Places that hold many memories for me over the decades, special places that I think about when I hit the stress threshold and want to escape to a less complicated world, places that I visualize, when I pause from fighting alligators at the office, and lean back in my chair, and close my eyes.

The first place I'm likely to think about is the ridge east of The Slash. It's the highest ridge on the island, and because it's the last one to go under in a flood, it has been the setting for more of my hunts than any other area on Ship Island.

*Original oil painting entitled **East of the Slash** by Norman C. Miller, Jr.*

I'm not quite sure how The Slash was named. I just remember hearing it called that from the early days of my childhood. I suppose the name derives from the fact that it is a relatively deep depression—for this part of the country, anyway—and is remarkably steep-sided on its east bank.

When you look at it on an aerial photograph, The Slash doesn't appear to be significant enough to have a name. Older aerials only reveal a line of woods running north and south that is slightly darker than the woods around it.

The Slash is more identifiable on later aerials, but only because a two-acre area opened up by a beaver-kill in the past 30 years is evident now.

The east bank of The Slash has one of the steepest slopes on the island. It was the "cutting bank" of the Mississippi River channel before the river changed course and the old channel was abandoned and silted-in more than 100 years ago. The vertical drop from the top of the high bank to the bottom of the Slash is nearly 15 feet, which puts it in the Grand-Canyon category for the Mississippi Delta.

When I was an inexperienced teenager, I learned an important lesson on this ridge. I learned to always set up as close as possible to the crest of the steep bank of a depression.

One day when I was with Kirk Biddle, I called a distant gobbler to our blind, which was situated 25 steps from the steep east bank of The Slash. We watched as the crafty old longbeard veered slightly to our left, slipped just under the high bank, and eased past us. He raised his head twice, just enough to get his eyeballs above the bank to check us out as he went by. We never got a shot at him.

It took more than one occasion like that to educate me. A couple of years later, in almost the same place on the ridge, I was again tutored by a gobbler. Although I didn't deserve it, I was luckier on that occasion. When the bird extended his head four inches above the crest of the bank, I knew it would be my only opportunity to take him.

When I shot, it looked as if someone had aimed a leaf-blower at the ground in front of the bird and had blown all the leaves and dirt away. I thought I had missed him, until I topped the high bank and saw him flopping near the edge of the water in the bottom of The Slash.

After twice seeing how effectively turkeys were able to use the steep east bank, the thought finally occurred to me that there was no reason why a hunter couldn't use it the same way.

Since then, I can't count the times I've used that east bank to get rounders on a gobbler. Unless the river is too high—above 30 to 31 feet at Memphis—which puts it too close to the top of the bank for me to stay out of view of turkeys on the ridge, I can easily slip unseen along the water's edge under the bank.

The west bank of The Slash, formerly the "towhead" side of the old riverbed, is much flatter in slope and slightly lower in elevation than the east side. For as long as I can remember, the ridge on the west side has been called Outhouse Ridge.

It's true that Outhouse Ridge was named for a real, honest-to-goodness outhouse. In the early 1950s some members of the old OK Hunting Club got the wild idea of having a deep-woods campout with some girl friends.

The campout was well organized. The members realized that the girls would not be as willing to rough it as the men, and would probably be hesitant to heed the calls of nature behind a tree. So, the scheming club members built a regulation-size, wood-frame outhouse on the wooded ridge to accommodate their presumably modest female guests.

For years after that, the old outhouse was a well-recognized landmark. It stood, near the bank of Tunica Cutoff Lake, through repeated floods, until it finally collapsed and fell during the 1973 flood.

For several years after it fell, you could still find a few weathered boards that marked the original site. Eventually rot took its toll, and the remnants of the revered old structure disappeared forever, except in the memories of the original OK Club members.

The timber on the ridge east of The Slash is neither the most picturesque nor the most valuable on the island. Box elder is far too prevalent in the stand. Box elder is in the maple family, but is a softer hardwood that timber companies hate to see marked for a timber sale. Usually there are only a handful of box elders in a stand that have one good log and decent form class.

A small area at the north end of the ridge was cut too heavily in a past logging operation, and has become somewhat overgrown with scrubby trees, spice bushes, and horseweeds. Thankfully, this area covers only about 10 acres. It's too thick in there to hunt, but I've set up many times on the periphery of it to call a gobbler.

Farther south on the ridge the timber stand improves, the average tree size increases, and the forest floor is more open. Large cottonwood and sycamore trees, most over 30 inches in diameter, stand like monoliths on this section of the ridge. Their abundance generally ensures that a hunter has an adequate choice of set-up trees.

Other common species on that section of ridge are

hackberry and American elm. The once-proud elm is one of our largest and most beautiful trees, but has been dying off for years because of a widespread fungal or viral disease. We see a few more dead ones every year.

A plethora of the wild turkey's preferred soft mast is available on the ridge, in the form of greenbriers, dewberries, wild grapes, yellow-tops, and other plants. Two of the principal mast-producing trees in our woods, sweet pecan and green ash, are uncommon on the ridge, however, and that probably explains why turkeys sometimes seem to use other areas of the island more when the river is lower.

The east high bank of The Slash itself is what potomologists, or river scientists, call a "natural levee," a levee formed by the dumping of heavier sand and loam particles suspended in a river when it overflows its banks.

The heavier particles are always the first to settle out in an overflow, which means that land near the bank builds to higher elevation than land more distant from the stream.

The results of this process are conspicuous along the east side of The Slash. Elevations are much higher on the east bank, and fall as you move east away from The Slash. The decline in slope is gradual, but not constant, across the breadth of the ridge.

In the central portion of the ridge the land begins to roll into a series of undulations the size of small ocean swells. From the peaks of these undulating "hog-back" ridges to the bottoms of the depressions between them are elevation changes of from six to eight feet, enough to conceal a man sneaking along to reposition himself on a gobbler.

*Cypress Brake on Ship Island*

This is the only place on the entire island that is remotely similar to hill terrain, where the chances of moving on a turkey are decent. Unfortunately, the area where these little ridges occur encompasses only about 30 acres, and the longest one is only about 1,200 feet long.

These little hogbacks are handy for slipping around on a turkey when the ridge is dry, but their greatest value is realized when the Mississippi River reaches a level of 32 to 33 feet on the Memphis river gauge. It is then that turkeys are highly concentrated east of The Slash.

The Big Bend area farther east is completely inundated by backwater at that gauge level, and turkeys there are forced up to the higher ground east of The Slash. The entire 30-acre, hog-back-ridge area transforms then into a series of long, narrow peninsulas, varying from 300 to 1,200 feet long and from 40 to 60 feet wide.

The longest and widest of these peninsulas is where several of my most exciting turkey-hunting memories were born. When the river is high enough and turkey populations are normal, I can always rely on a flock of turkeys, with at least one mature gobbler in it, being roosted just off the south tip of that peninsula. And the daily pattern of the birds using the peninsula is so dependable that I can practically use it as collateral at the bank. They always pitch down from the roost to the tip-end of the peninsula, then slowly strut and peck and feed their way north along it to where it joins the main ridge.

At that point, at the base of the peninsula, is where I'm always set up in a blind, waiting. Occasionally the birds will lift up and sail to another peninsula across the narrow scope of water separating the peninsulas, but this is somewhat uncommon.

I usually call periodically, to reassure the birds as they work their way up the peninsula toward me, but I'm not certain that it matters. In most cases, they probably would meander up to the main ridge anyway.

Another of my favorite places on the ridge is along the east high bank overlooking the bottom of The Slash. When the river rises, it backs into The Slash from the south. When the river at Memphis stands at 25 feet, a common level in the spring of the year, backwater extends two-thirds of the way up The Slash from our south line.

The point where the backwater ends is a tempting site for a midday or afternoon hunt, and I've set up there many times. In theory, this point would seem to be a strategic one, a sort of funnel through which turkeys moving from the ridge east of The Slash around to the Outhouse Ridge would have to pass, and vice-versa.

I know that turkeys move from one side of The Slash to the other, and since turkeys often prefer to feed along the edge of backwater, logic indicates they would have the tendency to travel around the head end of the water.

When I hunt in the afternoon, I often like to settle in one place and "set a spell," especially early in the season when the woods are more open. Since I have a tendency to doze off occasionally, I always build a thick blind to conceal my movement.

My favorite blind-up tree is a large, leaning box elder that stands only a couple of feet off the crest of the bank of The Slash. The tree has an angle of lean in it that maximizes comfort when I recline. That in itself is a find more precious than rubies. Ask any turkey hunter how often he's been able to find just the right tree at just the right spot to call from in his turkey-hunting career.

In most situations, the trees that are candidates for

*The Roman Road, along the ridge east of The Slash*

blind-up sites in a given area provide seating about as comfortable as a bag of baseball bats in a dugout. To avoid straddling large roots and leaning against six-inch-diameter grape vines, a hunter is usually forced to set up against a sapling about the diameter of a broom handle.

In addition to the relaxation afforded by my perfect tree, the place also has a comforting feel to it, a feeling of being in control, perched there on the high bank, 15 feet above the bottom of The Slash, like a guard in a watchtower.

When the river is at 25 feet, I always believe I'm going to kill a big gobbler when I set up there. It just looks too inviting, and the textbook says that I should.

Ironically, my special place on the high bank has to be filed under the heading of "favorite places to hunt where I've never killed a turkey." Even though I have an abiding faith that I'm going to kill a gobbler every time I set up there, I've yet to do so.

I know turkeys actually do migrate around the head end of the water there. I've seen their tracks in the mud. And, while set up farther away from The Slash on other occasions, I've worked turkeys that left me and walked around the water and over to Outhouse Ridge. The same thing has also happened to me in reverse, when I've worked birds on the Outhouse Ridge side.

My sleeping has nothing to do with it. I'm certain that a turkey has yet to sneak past me there while I was asleep, because I sleep lightly in the turkey woods. I would've heard a stick snap, or some other sound.

That leaves only one possible explanation for my dry runs there. My schedule just hasn't overlapped with a gobbler's yet. Nevertheless, I intend to continue scheduling some of my afternoon naps there.

There is another place in the center of the ridge east of The Slash where I like to set up in the afternoon. A 34-inch pecan tree stands north of a bend in the property line between us and the hunting club south of us, and it provides a broad backstop in case someone on the adjacent club decides to spray the area with shot.

The ridge is narrow there when the Memphis river gauge reads 25 feet. Not narrow enough for turkeys passing along the water's edge on either side of the tree to be within shotgun range, but narrow enough that a passing turkey can easily hear you calling from either side.

The woods are more open near the south line. The average tree size is large, and the resulting heavy canopy retards the understory growth, making the whole scene parklike. Such open woods require heavy blinding in the broad daylight of an afternoon hunt.

This is one of the few places where I ever build a Winn-class log blind. In years when I decide to use the site, I spend an hour or so early in the season constructing a fine log blind, then use it several times again during the season.

I build the blind up to eye level, and make it dense enough to conceal the wildest unconscious twitches that a sleeping hunter can make. The first longbeard I ever killed in the afternoon was taken from a log blind there.

Farther south on the ridge, down on Seabrook's land, is the spot where I killed my first turkey, a jake, on the old OK Club in 1960. Dad called it up for me, and I still remember him carving my initials in a tree near the spot where the jake fell.

That little ceremony made a lasting impression on me, and, ever since then, I've carved my name on a tree at the site of every one of my kills. And, following Dad's example, when my son Bob killed his first turkey, I carved his "B" on an Earnheartsville tree, too.

For years I cut my name into trees with a hunting knife. I felt compelled to cut a complete set of initials and the date into the tree each time. And, in the interest of being historically accurate, I would cut them into the tree nearest where the turkey fell, regardless of species. It usually took me about 30 minutes to complete the job, especially when a turkey fell by a pecan or sycamore tree. After a few years it became a chore.

One day several years ago, when Dad was cleaning out some old things, he gave me an old forester's tree scriber that had belonged to my grandfather. I conceived the idea of using the scriber to memorialize successful hunts, and it has made the job much easier.

I also shortened the whole process to about five minutes by leaving off the date and cutting a simple "W," and by only selecting softer trees, like box elders, to carve on.

I've had unforgettable hunts all over the ridge east of The Slash. I've doubled on gobblers with friends there more than anywhere else on the island. Billy Brookshire and I did it once, when he set up at the base of the main peninsula and killed a bird off the roost so quickly and easily that he called it a "layup."

Willie Green and I doubled twice on the ridge, in back-to-back years. Once I was part of a triple there on a cold morning with Willard McIlwain and Charlie Tindall.

All of these hunts occurred early in the spring season, when the river was high. The concentrating effect of the water contributed to the results, as did the fact that the hunts occurred early in the season before the turkeys had been pressured to excess.

Once when I brought my wife Becky hunting, we hunted at the head end of The Slash—in pouring rain, awful mosquitos, and at the end of the spring season, when the birds were through gobbling.

Conditions were the worst imaginable, but she sat patiently in the blind, reading while I called, then we gathered grape vines for wreaths when the hunt was over, as I had promised.

Becky hasn't been back, and I don't blame her. I've always regretted that she didn't have a decent opportunity to understand what a good turkey hunt is all about.

The ridge east of The Slash is indeed special, as is almost every corner of Ship Island. You don't ever see places like The Slash on Ship Island mentioned in the travel sections of magazines. Instead, they describe places with clear, rocky streams and mountains, or coastal areas with beaches that are as white as cane sugar.

But, I hope you have the opportunity one day to stroll along the east bank of The Slash. If you ever do, pause and examine the environment closely, and allow everything to soak in for a moment or two. What you'll see are shapes and colors that have beauty unrivaled in any other ecosystem you choose to compare them to.

Some would call it a swamp. I choose to call it a bottomland hardwood forest. There's just something about this type of forest that calms you and mercifully brings you back to life's basics.

I've never understood how anyone could reject the idea of God. I firmly believe that an afternoon spent beside The Slash, tuning-in to the miracles of creation there, would embolden the faith of any doubter.

The verdant lushness, the vivid colors of the wild flowers, the myriad variations in the flora and fauna, the timber, and the interaction between them all, are convincing signatures of our awesome Master Planner. If it's His will, next spring I'll be there celebrating Him again, on the ridge east of The Slash.